MW00577692

Over the years I have work
women in the Christian m
what one woman has made ... ...
it would have to be Barbie. Her talent is obvious, but talented people are everywhere (especially in Nashville). What sets Barbie apart as a teacher, songwriter, mother and wife is her passion and sincere love for the One from Whom her life and inspiration flows. Her sensitivity to spiritual things is obvious; she is always listening for God's voice - and they talk on a regular basis. I am blessed by the time I spend with her and I know you will be too."

Ed Kee, Director of A&R
Benson Records, Nashville TN

She is that all too rare person who lives consistent with what she teaches, but doesn't feel the need to lord that over others. She is always ready to grow in God's grace.

Barbie is an inspired teacher. She has the gift to bring a word that is both challenging and refreshing. She is in tune with the Spirit but solid and grounded. She will not leave you with a mess on your hands to clean up after. She has a joyful willing heart that is contagious.

Ronnie Meek, Senior Pastor
Springhouse Worship & Arts Center, Smyrna TN

Her profound humor and sincere love for the Word, along with her psalmist anointing, combine to make your time with her a *laughter-through-tears* experience. Barbie's passion for God will truly challenge you to press in deeper...and come up higher.

Frank and Barbara Price, Senior Pastors
Family Worship Center, Oliver Springs TN

Positioned for Transition

Arrows in His Hand

Positioned for Transition

Arrows in His Hand

By

BARBIE LOFLIN

WordCrafts

For my class at Springhouse

Your faithfulness and constant hunger keep me on my spiritual toes. Because you are willing to go there, I must forever dig deeper. I cannot imagine taking this journey without you. What a profound privilege to teach such amazing souls.

I love you guys so much!

For Sandi Accousti

My friend and editor, at large. I could not have done it without you. Thank you for your patience and generosity. Your presence in this process was God's gift to me.

Contents

Introduction

I am a *start at the beginning* kind of girl. Therefore, the only way I can possibly begin this journey with you is to share with you where it began with me.

I had been going through a season of extreme spiritual change. I can almost see the nodding of heads as many of you already understand. We have all been there. You think things are moving in a forward direction and you are pretty sure your feet are firmly planted in fair fields, with God directing your steps. Your life is going pretty good; the kids are not making you crazy; the "ministry" God has given you seems to be flowing; you are actually making forward progress in the things of the Spirit, and then, *Bam!* You wake up one morning and something has changed.

You're not quite sure what it is, but it has happened nonetheless. Your advancing world is somehow off-kilter; kind of like someone has shaved off your eyebrows while you slept. You haven't seen it yet, but you know a revelation is coming.

For me, what had actually changed was the satisfied feeling that had been a constant companion for the year and a half prior to this particular morning. I just woke up and felt frustrated. I couldn't put my finger on it. I just knew that God was getting ready to do something.

I know that feeling well. Something stirs on the inside of you, and though you would like to run you know it is not an option. Your personal history has proven you cannot outrun a God-stirring.

At that time I had been heavily involved in Women's Ministries and had taught weekly classes for several years. I had published three books in the prior year, and was busily working on the next two. There simply were not enough hours in the day. Still, I was content with everything that had taken place, and where the Lord had me. I had absolutely no desire to change anything.

Isn't that just the way it is? We're perfectly content when the ground begins to shake. I asked my mother one day why things had to get so messed up when God was trying to change things. She simply looked at me and said, "Well, honey, you would never move if things did not get uncomfortable where you were." I thought about what she said for some time after that. It was one of those moments that God uses over and over in our lives. I now immediately turn my eyes toward Him when I begin to feel unsettled, for many times it is He that is doing the unsettling work, moving me out of that spiritual easy chair.

Most of us do not like to think that our God of Love could possibly do anything that might make us uncomfortable or rock our world. After all, He is about happy thoughts and good feelings, running through flowery fields and laying beside still waters, right?

Unfortunately, or probably more accurately, disconcertingly, He is not only the God of the rainbow, but is also the God of the flood. I know, we like the rainbow-God, but the flood-God is awesome in His power, and it is wonderful to know that One such as this comes to your aid when you need Him most.

Anyway, as I was saying before I was sidetracked, I began to feel like something was up. Something was. In the weeks that followed, I could feel the drawing of God. He would awaken me in the night watches and call me to come and spend some time with Him in prayer. As I sought Him and His perfect will, He began to direct me to lay some things down. Not all of my *good* work was *God* work. Little by little He began to ask me to take some of the things off of my proverbial plate.

But I liked my plate. Everything fit perfectly and was pleasing to the eye. Alas, the plate was getting ready to tip, and even those things I thought securely in place were destined to topple.

First, He whispered to my heart that it was time for me to let go of women's ministries in our local body. What? *But, Lord, they need me!* (In actuality, I needed them.) This was hard. Though I knew God had placed wonderfully equipped women in the house for just such a moment, I wanted to hold on. You see, part of my identity was found in leading the women. All of a sudden this fear hit me that if I did not lead them, if I was not front and center, they would no longer need me - and I would be replaced in their hearts. I did not want to be replaced. Talk about having to deal with rejection issues!

How funny it is that God can hit so many targets with one tiny insecurity arrow. It's like the magic Kennedy bullet...so many places, so little time. Major ricochet.

Still, I knew it was God Who was speaking to my heart. I had no choice. You either do what God says, or you walk around with the rebellion "R" on your shirtfront (and unmistakably imprinted on the spirit). I did not want the R; for I know the limits it places on one's Kingdom potential.

I offered my insecurities to God as an offering, took up the cloak of surrender, and stepped down from the Women's Board. A wonderfully capable woman of God took the reins and lovingly steered the women in new directions; directions that did not pertain to me or my agendas. Miraculously (heavy sarcasm), God blessed that ministry without my ideas and input. In fact, they truly prospered without me. *Ouch!*

I licked my wounds for a few days and poured myself into my studies. *At least I still have my teaching. I will just throw myself into the Word and teaching.* My flesh settled down and peace came as I went to my absolute favorite place…the pages of the Word. Just when I became really comfortable, I felt the shaved eyebrows once again. I distinctly remember whispering toward the heavens, *You have got to be kidding!*

Have you ever tried to convince God that His idea is not a good one? For future reference, let me just settle that one for you…it doesn't work. I reasoned, explained, questioned and finally, tearfully submitted. I did leave with one final whine… *The women, I am sure, are already missing me, God! What will they do if I no longer teach them? I mean, God, I have been teaching in this church for 12 years!*

God has such a sense of humor. I know many might think that's a strange statement, but I have always found God to be so funny. Perhaps because I grew up in a home full of one-liners and profoundly sharp sarcasm, I have always sensed God's humor. I came to the conclusion a long time ago that

Satan could not possibly have anything to do with the wit and intelligence required to find the laughter in life. It could only be our creative God who birthed something this wonderful. Because of this mindset, I often feel that I get God's one-liners. He just runs them by me to see if I am listening closely enough.

When I said that I had been teaching for twelve years, I heard His unmistakable retort, "Well, then, don't you think it's past time for some new blood?"

Okay. This is not funny. My position (women's board) and my calling (teacher). What did I do? Why are you mad at me? What's next God, my passion (music)?

"Yes." (Never ask a question you do not really want the answer to.)

The laying down continued. No women's ministry, no teaching, no praise team. All I had left were my friends.

Et tu Bruté?

Yes, even my "fellowship" found itself shelved.

I remember thinking, *That's it! That's it, God! You want me to do nothing…well nothing is what I am going to do!*

I threw myself a wonderful pity party, with only myself in attendance. *After all,* I whined to God, *I obviously can't even have friends anymore!* Thus, the party began. I cried the ugly cry, sang all the verses to "Nobody Knows, the Trouble I've Seen," made sure the mascara lines marked my cheeks and took a mental picture of my profound suffering for Christ. As I lay there on the living room sofa, t-shirt stained by melted ice cream, two empty bottles of root beer rolling around on the floor, vacant Pringles can now holding my

Almond Joy and beef jerky wrappers, Aretha Franklin blaring in the background, R-E-S-P-E-C-T, I came to the conclusion...*I throw a pretty good party!*

No, in all seriousness, I did make a decision. It would be a decision that would put me on my face before God and take all of the *I want's* out of my vocabulary.

My decision? I decided that I was not going to stay at the party. I decided that I still trusted God enough to give Him my life...and all of my stuff. I decided that I truly did believe He loved me...loved me extravagantly and lavishly. I knew He had to have a plan for me; a great one...and I decided I wanted to be a part of whatever He had planned.

I got off the sofa, brushed my road-kill hair, and went looking for my prayer journals. I needed to remind myself of all that He had been saying. I had to find out if I had missed something. I had to find God's heart, and in doing so, find new direction for my life.

I truly began to seek God as to what was actually going on. Novel idea, huh? When the whining, tears and chocolate no longer do it for you, you just may want to talk to God and get some answers from Someone Who knows.

One day while just talking to Him as I cleaned, I simply said, *Father, can you just show me where I am in this journey?* In the blink of an eye my spirit opened to what I can only call a vision. I still knew where I was. I did not black out or lose consciousness, but I very clearly saw something that was not there in the physical.

Before me stood a warrior in profile. His forearms were encased in leather, and there were sandals on his feet. His tunic was rough and nondescript, and across his back was a quiver full of arrows. In His left hand he held a bow. I watched as he reached back over his shoulder and retrieved one of the arrows, swinging it over his head, bringing it down toward the earth before locking it upon the bow. When the arrow was securely in place, The Archer began to lift the bow and arrow, bringing it up into alignment. Left arm taut, The Archer looked down the length of the arrow and lined up his shot. He then drew the arrow completely back, bringing it in line with his mouth and his ear. Up to this point, there had been no words, merely a watching of movement and positioning. But when the arrow was fully drawn back and rested close to his mouth and ear, The Archer finally spoke. He said three words, "You are here."

It was one of those moments that you can't really put into words, but those three words were full of revelation and they resounded through my spirit like a bowling ball in a glass house. They messed me up. They rocked my world and stirred me as nothing had stirred me in a long time.

I couldn't let it go. The picture, the image, the words, the revelation. I knew there was so much more to it, for with every movement of The Archer's hand and every movement of the arrow, I saw something in my spirit. You see, God doesn't have to speak audible words in order to get His point across. The Archer awakened me - the slumbering me I hadn't even known was asleep.

The teacher in me raised her head once again, and I sat down and asked the Father to take me through the process, showing me step-by-step everything I had seen. I asked Him to open my eyes and reveal to my spirit all that He had shown me in that one moment.

Pen in hand, journal before me, He began to teach me (Oh, how I love when He does this!) about the life of an arrow; more specifically, the life of an Arrow in His Hand.

In the following pages, I take you on the journey – from hand to target and back again. My prayer is that God will use this to reveal His work in your current positioning in the Kingdom. May you be encouraged and strengthened as you find your place and may hope bring you to a place of great obedience, as you submit to The Archer's hand.

Positioned for Transition

ARROWS IN HIS HAND

Positioned For Transition

He gave me speech that would cut and penetrate. He kept his hand on me to protect me. He made me his straight arrow and hid me in his quiver.

Isaiah 49:1-3

Becoming is a process. As cool as it might be to think about jumping from one phase of our lives directly into the next, the reality of such a thing is not quite so wonderful. I have come to see life as a series of small steps on a long and beautiful pathway. On each step you find instructions which tell you how to move onto the next step. Each step carries wisdom for the journey. We progress as we follow the instructions and gain the wisdom of the step.

Still, there is the temptation to skip steps when we gain a little wisdom. We think we should be able to move from here to there in a much shorter time. We think we know where we are going and have no need of the small step by step instructions.

Pure folly, my friend.

To skip steps implies that we know where and what the next step is. Not smart. As much as we would like to know what God is doing before He does it, it just doesn't work that way. He has a tendency to hide the next step until we are firmly planted on the current one. We know human steps and fleshly wisdom, but God is not human, and He is not limited by flesh. We step, and move in inches. He steps, and moves in levels and dominions.

Something that just may help you along the way is this little revelation: *God is all about the journey.*

We are the ones who long for the destination. We just want to get there. He wants us to experience the lessons of the path. He wants us to see the sights, feel the wind on our face, run through the green pastures, lay beside the still waters, marvel at the lightning, and stand in awe as the thunder rumbles off in the distance. If we run down this path, we might the Samaritan work God has for us. We may miss the wounded soul we were supposed to minister to; or worse yet, ignore them in our haste to arrive. Yes, God is about the journey.

Before we go any further, I would like for you to take a moment and consider where you think you might be in the phases of the instruction of an arrow.

Are you still trying to figure out if you have been chosen? Do you feel invisible, hidden away and unseen? Perhaps you are in the midst of testing, and are still finding out about yourself and about The Archer. You might be fully drawn back, ready to fly at any moment. Or you may find yourself as a facedown arrow, just finding divine humility at His feet.

Make no mistake, we are on a journey, and try as we might, we cannot escape from it. The sweet beckoning from the other side demands that we get to Him, and the journey is the only thing that stands between us. It is the great imperative that we set our hearts fully and joyfully on this pilgrimage and not look back.

Where are you in the journey? Are you progressing or digressing? Are you learning what you need to learn so that you may go where you need to go and accomplish all that you have been designed and destined to accomplish?

When the Lord began to give me this particular teaching regarding the Arrows, I spent a great deal of time in prayer. I did not want to move out and presume to know what He was talking about (remember, the whole step by step thing). I literally walked through each and every step time after time. I really wanted to search His heart in this. I wanted to understand the process. I did not want the head knowledge, I wanted heart-conviction. I had to know that this was truth-revealed. I did not want to teach a formula (we have a million of those), but share a revelation from His Word.

I do not know how to do that other than to lay out before Him in prayer. I went prostrate before Him in my office floor (I've become quite accustomed to carpet imprints on my forehead), and sought Him with all of my heart. I stayed in that prayerful posture before Him. Bible open, Spirit seeking, I asked Him to show me all that I needed to see. I asked Him to open my eyes, and enlighten my spirit.

Did you know it is okay to ask for wisdom and revelation?

That's why, when I heard of the solid trust you have in the Master Jesus and your outpouring of love to all the followers of Jesus, I couldn't stop thanking God for you - every time I prayed, I'd think of you and give thanks. But I do more than thank. I ask - ask the God of our Master, Jesus Christ, the God of glory - to make you intelligent and discerning in knowing him personally, your eyes focused and clear, so that you can see exactly what it is He is calling you to do, grasp the immensity of this glorious way of life

3

He has for His followers, oh, the utter extravagance of His
work in us who trust Him - endless energy, boundless
strength!

Ephesians 1:15-19

You see, God wants us to have wisdom and to be open to
revelation. Why? So we can impress our friends and become
self-inflated? No. He wants to show us things and have us
understand them for one purpose - that we might know Him
better.

That's where I went. I began to pray and fast, seeking Him
in earnest for wisdom and revelation. If I was going to make
even the most feeble attempt to give others a glimpse of His
heart in these matters, I needed to know Him better.

Oh, friend, do you grasp the wonderful access we have to the
Father? He hears every prayer offered from a sincere heart,
and He answers; not always as we would have desired, but
always as is best. Knowing this, I laid my petition before
Him. I cried out for understanding and sought wisdom. I
asked Him to reveal Himself as The Archer to this heart. I
asked Him to help me see the work of The Archer and the
arrow through His eyes.

Somewhere between desperation and elation, I found His
Warrior footprints, and began to follow.

When I asked my question of the Lord, I was actually hoping
for a diagram and graphs. Instead, what He began to show
me was an internal working that would be addressed by this
study. Instead of *the what*, He began to show me *the why*.

God began to open my heart to the frustration He sees in
His people. There are so many who have become frustrated
with the process of becoming whatever it is they feel they are

supposed to become. They are weary of the journey. They are just so tired of feeling like they gain spiritual ground only to turn around and lose their footing. They are losing heart because they cannot see any gaining of ground. They feel like they are doing the same things over and over and never getting anywhere. They feel as if they are spiritually running in place. We all know that will absolutely wear you out!

Beyond that, there are those who have no idea that they are actually on a journey, and that they really do have somewhere to go with God. To these, salvation is the beginning and the end. They are destination seekers. That's okay, if all you want to do is get there. You can still get there. But wouldn't you like to be fully awake for the journey? Wouldn't you like to learn everything you could possibly learn, to be constantly filled and refilled with His spirit, to live richly, wetly, and accomplish all you were supposed to accomplish on the planet?

I believe that if we do what we were supposed to do, and grow in Him, our children will have a wonderfully rich inheritance. I believe that my children can use my highest point as their jumping off place. My ceiling should be their floor. My journey should give them a great point of reference, allowing them to advance the Kingdom to a much greater extent than I ever could. My effective journey affects theirs. My prayer is that my children would far surpass me in all spiritual matters and levels of fullness and wisdom. They will not do that if I refuse to take my journey, if I merely wait for eternity to overtake me.

And we're here today bringing you good news: the Message that what God promised the fathers has come true for the children...

Acts 13:32-33

But, I digress. I did not mean to go there. Back to our subject matter.

As I sought the Lord an image began to form in my mind: arrows in a field, arrows in various positions; all in preparation for use by The Archer. Waiting... waiting for The Mighty Warrior to take them into His hand.

Oh, that stirs me up! God wants to use us. We are literally arrows in His hand. He wants to use us to advance His kingdom in the earth. He wants to prepare us, equip us and send us flying into the center of His will. He has wonderful plans for our lives. Friend, do you understand that you have been uniquely and intricately designed for a life of fruitfulness, fulfillment, productivity, usefulness? God has placed a calling on your life, and it is a calling of great impact. You are being positioned for transition.

For I know the plans I have for you," declares the LORD, "plans to prosper you and not to harm you, plans to give you hope and a future. Then you will call upon me and come and pray to me, and I will listen to you. You will seek me and find me when you seek me with all your heart.
Jeremiah 29:11-13

Honestly, if you are not interested in the mark God has for you to hit in this life, you probably just need to lay this book down and walk away. This book is not for those who are content to sit back and watch others progress on their journey, never sensing a pull in their own spirits to move forward. If this is you, seriously, put the book down and turn the television back on. You are going to truly mess up your "happy place" if you delve any further. You will not hunger for *more*, if *more* has never been presented as an option. Oh, and my friend, not only do I intend to offer you the option of *more* in the spirit, but of *higher, faster, fuller*, to present to you the absolute promise of *flight*!

There is God-breath in the room as your foot touches this pathway and you find His hand surrounding the arrow. God is at work in your life even as you read these pages. He is moving you, shifting you into preordained places at this very moment, and eternity is exploding with the expectancy of your imminent release.

Oh friend, truly this is not for those who are still wondering if they can be used by God. This is for those who already know He is going to; who just know God has a purpose for all of this training they have been going through and submitting to. You know the drawing of "something altogether other" and you are ready to be about it! You know you have a calling on your life. You just are not sure where you are in the process of touching it and moving out into it.

Well, call me a fringe-dweller, but I have just enough faith to believe that the Holy Spirit is absolutely going to show you where you are positioned in this journey, and He is going to show you in the most simple and profound of ways; by giving you a glimpse of Himself (The Archer) and of yourself (The Arrow). I believe He is going to reveal to you not only where you have been and why you have had to go through what you have gone through, but will also give you a glimpse of your greater purpose and calling. Yes, I believe you will find your own journey in the journey of the Arrow, and in doing so, will learn to be patient in times of preparation, so that you will have the insight and vision needed to strike the mark when fully released by The Archer.

In other words, I believe God is going to do exactly what scripture says He will do: *...give you a spirit of wisdom and revelation, so that you may know Him better.* For, you see, God is looking for those who are willing to be chosen, hidden, exposed, humbled, exalted, positioned, drawn back, instructed and released to advance the Kingdom of God in the earth.

Is this you? Are you hungry for wisdom and revelation? Do you long to be used by God to impact the world?

Is there a stirring within you to know Him better? Do you long to truly experience His presence, and recognize His voice? Are you divinely frustrated?

Is your spirit quickened, and are your emotions raw? Do you vacillate between laughter and tears, as your heart knows the calling to deeper waters? Do others seem to resent you for believing God is going to use you? Have you passed the point of caring what they think, and moved into being fully focused on what pleases Him?

Has the enemy increased his reminders of past failures?

If so, rejoice! He has positioned you for transition. You are sublimely, frustratingly uncomfortable with the stagnancy in your walk with Christ. You can already feel the deeper stirring, sense the higher call, and smell the fragrance of God in your nostrils. You stand on the very precipice of awaiting wonder.

Dear One, it is time. Allow Him do what only He can do. Let Him blow away your perceptions of why you were placed on this planet. It is time to open your spirit to the possibility (and probability) that you are a beautifully polished arrow in the hand of an Omnipotent God. You have much to accomplish in the earth. You have great purpose and many marks to strike. You have been created for many destinations, and the journey begins with one simple prayer: Father, make me an arrow in your hand.

And the adventure begins.

Chosen

So, chosen by God for this new life of love, dress in the wardrobe God picked out for you: compassion, kindness, humility, quiet strength, discipline.
Be even-tempered, content with second place, quick to forgive an offense.
Forgive as quickly and completely as the Master forgave you. And regardless of what else you put on, wear love. It's your basic, all-purpose garment. Never be without it.
                                                                    Colossians 3:12

My husband is an archer. A good one. So, when the Father began to speak to my heart about the journey of an arrow, I began to watch my husband more closely when it came to his preparation process. Even the smallest thing became revelatory to me. Things I once overlooked and thought unimportant were suddenly glaringly profound. God was opening my spirit to receive insight of the spiritual through the physical. He does this to me a lot. If you pay close attention to what is going on around you, you will find God speaking to you in the most ordinary of situations. The sixty-fifth Psalm gives us a wonderful example of God's work as witnessed in the natural earth:

Blessed are the chosen! Blessed the guest at home in your place! We expect our fill of good things in your house, your heavenly manse. All your salvation wonders are on display in your trophy room. Earth-Tamer, Ocean-Pourer, Mountain-Maker, Hill-Dresser, Muzzler of sea storm and wave crash, ... Dawn and dusk take turns calling, "Come and worship."

Oh, visit the earth, ask her to join the dance! Deck her out in spring showers, fill the God-River with living water. Paint the wheat fields golden. Creation was made for this! Drench the plowed fields, soak the dirt clods With rainfall as harrow and rake bring her to blossom and fruit. Snow-crown the peaks with splendor, scatter rose petals down your paths, All through the wild meadows, rose petals. Set the hills to dancing, Dress the canyon walls with live sheep, a drape of flax across the valleys. Let them shout, and shout, and shout! Oh, oh, let them sing!

Psalm 65:4-13

As a case in point, I would like to share with you an example of God taking an ordinary moment and teaching an extraordinary lesson. He is marvelous at this! He opens our natural eyes and gives us glimpses of the supernatural. I know you have all had those moments when you saw something you might have normally overlooked, simply because He gave you a new perspective on something so very ordinary and simple it had become mundane.

One Wednesday evening I was running a little late for church. I had headed out to the car and backed out of the garage, still waiting on my daughter, Kaitlen. (This was no surprise. I often found myself waiting on this child.) Katie, about 7 years old at the time, came rushing out to the car after an extended wait on my part. When she finally plopped down in the car, purses, bags and books flying across the seat,

I said, "Kaitlen, where have you been? I have been sitting here waiting for you."

A look came across her face that clearly said, *you are not going to believe what I have been through!* Her little voice turned serious, "I'm sorry, Mama. I was coming through the kitchen, and when I turned around, my bag knocked a soda off the counter and coke went everywhere!"

I nodded, understanding now. "Oh, okay," I said, ready now to back out of the drive.

She then rolls her eyes and says, "Just imagine how long it would have taken me if I had stayed in there to clean it up!"

I hit the brakes. The mom part of me – the part that knows how much work it is to find all of the potentially sticky residue - wanted to go off; after all, she had left a mess because she knew I would come behind her and clean it up! About the time the accusation started to pass my lips, God's Spirit inside of me gently spoke: *Barbie, you do this all of the time. You make a mess and walk away from it. You ask me to forgive you and just keep walking. Sometimes you have to go back and clean up the mess.*

In that moment, God reminded me of some issues that needed attention, some apologies that needed to be made - my own coke-messes left for someone else to deal with.

Needless to say, Kate and I made a little trip back into the house and spent a little quality time in the kitchen. Later that evening, the Father and I spent some quality time of our own talking about some of my own messes, things I needed to make right, instead of just walking away and expecting grace.

Though it may seem a bit off-subject, this is an example of spiritual revelation birthed of ordinary stuff. You must begin to look for it. Be heightened in your capacity to discern the miraculous in all that is around you. God is constantly speaking, but sadly, our hearing has become so very dull. We must start listening more attentively.

Why am I going here? What does seeing the miraculous in the mundane have to do with this study? It's really very simple: If you are going to get what you need to get out of this ordinary study, you are going to have to see the potentially miraculous in it. You're going to have to see it through God's eyes. You are going to have to reach beyond the words on page, and see the revelation God is trying convey to our limited flesh.

I believe He is trying to give us a tool with which we can determine where we are in the journey, so that we might better know how to learn the lessons of each phase in order to move forward. As you study the stages of the instruction of the arrow, look deeper. Allow the Holy Spirit to reveal deeper truth; truth that has nothing to do with what you think you see, feel or know. Allow room for personal, Word-backed revelation. It will make all of the difference.

Now that we have that settled, let's move onward and upward.

In my search for the *super* in the *natural*, I started paying attention when Hal would have boxes delivered to the front door. One day I stuck around and watched as he opened a box and started taking his arrows out, one by one. (My husband has always been extremely meticulous. He is an absolute detail person. I often think that God must have given him a double portion of the gift of administration because He knew the man was going to have to deal with me. He knew how desperately I would need that gift to come alongside!) In all honesty, I had not realized what intricate inspection takes place in the choosing of an arrow. I merely assumed if it was an arrow (stick, feathers and pointy thing – love the technical terminology), it would be used.

Wrong.

In fact, a good arrow does not even receive its razor tip until time for its first flight! Think about the implications of that for a moment.

I watched my husband, Hal, begin to separate the arrows. First he laid them out side by side to check their length and measured each. He obviously knew what was required and was looking for those that met the requirements. God is like that, you know. When He examines us He is looking for specific things; things we will need on our assignment. He is the only One Who knows what will be required of us.

In retrospect, I find it quite interesting to think that all of the things I thought would be needed for my journey have truly had very little to do with it. The things that once were so important to me, no longer are. And the things I once overlooked, have become jewels - my truest treasure.

God's criteria are so different. He chooses you based on things like your ability to extend grace, a propensity for mercy, fierce humility, and a tender, teachable heart.

What? You mean it has nothing to do with my vast knowledge of the scripture, astounding gifts, height, ability, weight, hair color, gifts, square footage of my house or even the kind of car I drive? Nope! Nothing of the kind.

God searches hearts, not resumes.

Here I go again, jumping off the track toward *Chosen*. Sorry.

I spent a lot of years trying (and failing) to get someone to pick me in one manner of another. I have four beautiful, talented sisters, and finding your niche in their shadows can be really difficult. Angie was the fragile, pretty one. Teresa – brilliant and definitely the coolest. Cindy- compassionate, generous, unbelievable physique, and the absolute sweetest. Melody, dark hair, olive skinned perfection.

And there I was, right in the middle: clumsy, red hair, freckles and really big feet, and a tomboy to beat all tomboys.

To say that my sisters outshone me would be a vast understatement. It once made me extremely self-conscious; it now makes me fabulously proud! They are wonderful, insightful, gifted daughters of God, and they literally buckle my knees with their humor. There are very few left standing when their combined intellects and humor enter the room. Yes, they are still beautiful, and I am okay with that. I no longer strive with myself, for there are far too many willing to do that for me. I have truly come to embrace our differences, and finally found my place (and my peace) in my Beloved. He is enamored with me, you know, and I with Him. He levels all playing fields with one captivated glance.

Dear Sojourner, it is important that you know God is not looking at what you think He is looking at. Beyond that, His eyes are so filled with love that even those things He does see, He sees completely differently than you do. He thinks you are wonderful. He made you just as you are.

He picked you!

Okay, back to the arrows. Next Hal picked up each arrow and checked it from every angle. He checked the fletching

15

(feathers), carefully running his hands along its length. He did not assume that all was in order based on sight. He had to get his hands on it to examine it for ultimate use. He had to make sure that the arrow was capable of flying true, of striking the intended mark. Those arrows that did not meet inspection criteria were set aside.

Though I was a little hesitant to interrupt his perusal of the arrows, I asked, "Are you going to throw the bad ones out?"

What he said struck me.

"No," he said. "I will see if they can be reshaped."

He did not discard even those that had an obvious flaw. Even though he could not use them at this time, he was going to work with them to bring them into a useful state.

Can you say, "Thank You, Jesus!"

Oh, friend, I am that reshaped arrow! Actually, I am a multiple re-shaper. What about you? I think the Father must reshape this arrow on a daily basis. I am forever trying to bend in my own directions. What He has taught me in this process is that prayer will keep me tender and pliable in His hand, while His Word makes the needed adjustments. But for that to happen I must stay immersed in His Word, and our lines of communication must remain open and fluid at all times.

Yes, my shaky arrow, you are going to feel under a microscope during this phase of your instruction. Chosen, you are being searched on every level.

During this phase, a key stabilizing component must remain in place: we must be conscious about our propensity for attributing human motives to God. People often scrutinize

16

in order to make themselves feel better by comparison. God has no such motive. Everything He reveals is for our healing, not for our utter shame and mortification. God's revelation of our misshapen form is for no reason other than our healing and redemption from it. His revelation is always for our eternal benefit. This is not to be mistaken with condescending tones and imperiously raised eyebrows, giving voice to pretentiously benevolent whispers of, *I'm telling you this for your own good.*

Oh, please. Spare me that kind of good!

Remember this: God's revelation of weakness brings the promise of His strength. Your enemies' revelation brings hopelessness and shame. You can easily discern between the two.

Another caution: make sure you do not let yourself feel overwhelmed when the Father begins to bring things to the surface. Trust Him to help you deal with whatever issues may arise. He loves you completely, and He is fully dedicated to seeing you whole and healthy. Do not let yourself believe anything that does not line up with that certainty of thought.

It is imperative during this phase of instruction that you follow the precepts laid out in a familiar passage of scripture:

> *Celebrate God all day, every day. I mean, revel in him! Make it as clear as you can to all you meet that you're on their side, working with them and not against them. Help them see that the Master is about to arrive. He could show up any minute!*
> *Don't fret or worry. Instead of worrying, pray. Let petitions and praises shape your worries into prayers, letting God know your concerns. Before you know it, a*

17

sense of God's wholeness, everything coming together for good, will come and settle you down. It's wonderful what happens when Christ displaces worry at the center of your life.

Summing it all up, friends, I'd say you'll do best by filling your minds and meditating on things true, noble, reputable, authentic, compelling, gracious – the best, not the worst; the beautiful, not the ugly; things to praise, not things to curse. Put into practice what you learned from me, what you heard and saw and realized. Do that, and God, who makes everything work together, will work you into his most excellent harmonies.

Philippians 4:4-9

You must keep your mind and spirit controlled during your "examination" time. Otherwise, the enemy will take conviction and make it look and feel like condemnation. We want the former, not the latter; for one reshapes and one destroys. Have a God-view of your failures and shortcomings, for in doing that, grace and new mercies always arrive on the scene. From this, you step into repentance, not repetition.

Make sense? Our goal during this time is to come to Job's revelation - without Job's trials.

"But he knows where I am and what I've done. He can cross-examine me all he wants, and I'll pass the test with honors. I've followed him closely, my feet in his footprints, not once swerving from his way. I've obeyed every word he's spoken, and not just obeyed his advice – I've treasured it."

Job 23:10

As I watched my husband examine the arrows, I could not help but feel a little bit of sorrow for the arrows that were set aside. I know they are inanimate objects, but as I was looking for the miraculous in the mundane God was teaching me about arrows as they pertain to His children. Each arrow my husband held in his hand had been created and shaped for flight, just as each of us has been created for specific purpose. When one was not chosen for use, my heart hurt a bit. I had to remind myself that each would have the opportunity to be reshaped and made useful. A skilled archer knows how to handle an arrow and realign it (trust me in this!).

God spoke gently to my spirit, "All of the arrows have been chosen: one chosen for use, another chosen for shaping, and still another chosen for further inspection. None have been discarded; their release will come at various times."

Your release, my friend, will come at times that differ from that of your friends, family members, mate's, etc. Do not think you have missed it or messed up simply because someone close to you takes flight before you do. Apply yourself to His instructions and let The Archer do His work. Did you ever consider that the mark you were intended to strike may not be ready for you yet?

I watched Hal pick up the arrows that had passed inspection. I knew a moment's excitement as I watched him walk out the back door and head for the area where he tests the arrows, for I knew the arrow was getting ready to fly for the first time.

A shaft of jealousy ran through me. How I wanted to fly! I know, I can be so silly when God is showing me something, but my flesh just responds to the stirring in my spirit. You see, I know first flights are amazing, scary, awesome, nerve

19

wracking, elation invoking, hope inducing, wondrous things! Something inside of me longed to be the arrow in his hand. I wanted to be the one he had chosen to use. It was a cry from my spirit, not my head.

In faith, I caught a glimpse of future flight, right before I heard the spirit-whisper that rocked me: "You are My arrow, and you will soar alongside the great."

I knew that whisper. I knew that voice. And I knew the promise was one that had echoed through the ages, touching king and pauper alike; it was a call and promise to all of His arrows. It was the awakening and drawing of God-potential in the life of the sons and daughters of Adam.

I also knew that *great* is defined differently in the kingdom of God. In the Kingdom, the greatest are the least, and the servant is most like the Son. Oh my friend, I long for that kind of greatness; the kind of greatness that dries tears away, and holds the broken in arms of kindness, the kind that extends hands and cradles generations safely within the knowledge of a good and faithful God.

What about you? Are you ready to enter into a new level of greatness? Are you ready to trade your aspirations for His hopes, your plans for His purposes? So much awaits you beyond this door of decision, the door clearly marked, *Less of me, More of You.*

Yes, there are times when all undergo the examination of The Archer. In our flesh, we may feel like we are being judged, criticized and scrutinized, when in fact we are being prepared for use. Big difference. Huge difference. Scrutiny for the sake of comparison and judgment is like a beauty pageant where you never make the top twenty. You are picked apart and found wanting. We have all been there at least a thousand times. It is painful, demeaning, degrading and often humiliating to be found lacking in someone's sight.

Ah, but God is not examining with intent to reject. He is examining like one who would check the equipment of a soldier; making sure they have everything needed for battle right before stepping onto the battlefield. He examines closely because His love is great. His need to protect you makes Him very thorough in His perusal. The desire to see that you have all you need is His primary motivation. Do you see the difference? One examination shames, while the other equips.

My arrow friend, I joyfully submit to His examination, His preparatory searching, in order that I might be better prepared for the battle - and the victory.

One other thing I would like for you to be keenly aware of during this phase of instruction is this:

> *The king is enthralled by your beauty; honor him, for he is your lord.*
>
> Psalm 45:11

In the midst of this process, never forget how much He loves you. Never let go of His fragrance. Know that you are precious to Him, and nothing is going to take you out of His hand. Even the reshaping is done in the center of and by His beautiful hands. Do not lose sight of God's love. Do not waiver from your conviction that you are the apple of His eye.

I believe it is during this part of the process that God is determining *when*, not *if*, the arrow will be used. Do not reject or resent His close examination. Submit to His hand and lean into His instruction. There is a greater work being accomplished, and an intricate and eternal testing is taking place. What is He testing us in? Well, we actually read some criteria at the very beginning of this session:

So, chosen by God for this new life of love, dress in the wardrobe God picked out for you: compassion, kindness, humility, quiet strength, discipline. Be even-tempered, content with second place, quick to forgive an offense. Forgive as quickly and completely as the Master forgave you. And regardless of what else you put on, wear love. It's your basic, all-purpose garment. Never be without it.

Colossians 3:12

I believe this is a specific directive when it comes to this phase of the journey. With the knowledge of being chosen by God for this new life, we must begin the process of being transformed by the renewing of our minds. If you are looking for indicators and signposts that tell you where you are in the progression toward your mark, begin to pay close attention to your walk in the following areas. You will see changes taking place once you begin to find your place of rest in being His Chosen.

Are you compassionate? Do you find yourself being sympathetic and having a consciousness of others' distress coupled with a desire to alleviate it?

Do you see changes in your heart which compel you to move in kindness on a completely different level?

Are you checking your pride issues; walking in new places of humility?

22

Have you developed a sort of quiet strength which takes away your need to prove yourself to those around you?

What about discipline? Is your prayer life becoming more regulated, your time in the Word as regular as breathing?

Temper issues should be diminishing; acts of the selfish nature are becoming less frequent. As an ambassador of Christ you begin to make every effort to comport yourself in ways that honor Him and bring glory to His name. Dying to the selfish compulsion to prove your point is an absolute must in this phase.

Are you content with second place? Can you serve in hidden positions where no one notices your service except you and God? What if The Archer determines you will always serve in hidden positions? Can you lay it all down and serve with joyful abandon in the hidden places? Do you have to be up front, or can you just be purely obedient (and content) wherever He places you?

Finally, are you quick to forgive offenses? Can you truly let things go and move forward without a chip on your shoulder? Are you willing to lay down an offense without ever confronting the issue or the person? Can you forgive not because you have received an apology, but simply because it is God's will?

These are some of the primary characteristics of the Chosen. These are outward manifestations of a deep inner work. Issues like these must be worked out during your time in His hand. If you are genuinely interested in what The Archer is looking for as He examines the arrow, take an honest look at these things, for I can tell you a good human arrow has these characteristics.

Ah, but even during the close scrutiny, remember, you are safely in His hand. Know the warmth of His touch, the love in His gaze. Hold nothing back and keep nothing hidden. Allow Him access to all that you are. Relax into Him. Be content to stay in His hand, no matter what the outcome. Do not give in to the urge to ask Him to hurry. Be content to have found your way into His hand. It is enough. It is more than enough.

I have found that once held in His hand, little else matters. Just drawing in this close to Him changes who you are. You know a completely different dimension of peace. In fact, many of us can get stuck here. I am guilty of holding on in this place. We just do not want to leave the safety of His hand. We like knowing He is a breath away. We feel sheltered, comfortable and extraordinarily special… perhaps for the first time in our lives. We can become so caught up in the intimacy of this place that we refuse to allow ourselves to be moved into the next phase of preparation. While it is a wonderful thing to know you have His full attention and to experience the sweetness of His touch, it is the assurance of His touch that should actually birth within us the strength (and desire) to take our place wherever His hand might next move.

Before we go any further, can I just tell you that I love this step in the process? This is the time when I feel like I am Daddy's girl and I have His complete attention. I may not be ready for flight, but it does not seem to matter while in His presence. Before one life-altering flight, I actually spent about two years in this particular phase of instruction. It wasn't that I had not learned to submit, it was that I fell in love with that place in Him. I was content to stay and never move out of that *shadow-of-His-wings* kind of intimacy.

He allowed me to stay there because He knew there was healing that needed to take place in the depths of this misshapen arrow. Even after being healed, He allowed me to stay beyond what was needed, merely because I found such fulfillment there.

You see, God is about more than healing. He is an extravagant God Who loves to bless His children - just because He can. He knew that this abandoned little girl's heart just longed for daddy-time. Could I have moved forward without the extra? Sure. But I have made a wonderful discovery in my advancing years: God is all about the extra.

Now hear me: I am not talking about temporal goodies and prayer-order God-fluff. I am talking about a God who awakens the eternity written upon your heart, but does not stop there. He starts to breathe over it, nurture it in His hand and then showers your greatest potential with living waters, causing it to spring up and break loose like a wild thing. He is lavish in His already extravagant love.

Oh, do you get it? He chooses you, takes you into His hand, examines you, heals you, prepares you and then waits until you are ready to move to the next phase of instruction. Ah! Who does this? There is no other God like this!

He was so very patient with me during this phase. He allowed me to stay in a place of deep intimacy for two years...I mean Holy Place intimacy. He let me hide and soak, let me dream and bask, until I was ready to head into the next phase of instruction. He waited for me to tell Him I was ready, and then gently brought me out into the next phase.

What I have come to realize is that I was only able to move forward when I understood I could run back to that place with Him if I needed. Intimacy with Him is an open invitation, not an earned privilege. I now run to Him at will, and He always opens His arms wide. You will find that in all phases of the instruction of the arrow, His hand will always hold you and shape you in one way or another.

Yes, you have been chosen by God, with a very specific purpose in mind. You are an arrow coming fully and confidently into His hand.

> *For we know, brothers loved by God, that he has chosen you, because our gospel came to you not simply with words, but also with power, with the Holy Spirit and with deep conviction.*
>
> I Thessalonians 1:4-5 (NIV)

If you need to settle this issue, I want you to look at three things presented in the above verses and ask yourself about your deliverance from darkness into light. The Word says in these things you will know that He has chosen you: (not to be mistaken with salvation issues).

Did the gospel come to you with power? (When you heard the Word and received the Truth, was it as if you finally came alive in the depths of your being?)

Did the Holy Spirit fill you and change you? (Are you becoming a new creation in Him? Have you become new?)

Do you know the correction and conviction of God deep within your spirit? (Are you learning to sense His presence and listen for His direction? Has your sensitivity to what is right and wrong increased?)

Have you asked Jesus Christ to be your personal Savior, acknowledging and believing that He was and is the sinless Son of God? Have you begun to experience the power, the Spirit, the change, the correction and conviction of God? If so, you can know beyond a shadow of a doubt that you have been chosen by God.

But then, the issue is not really whether or not you have been chosen, is it? The issue is whether or not you truly believe that God wants to use your life to change the lives of others. You need His revelation to know that Truth. You need to be able to settle the *can God really use me* question. Beyond that, you must be able to accept the truth of the situation; not only *can* He use you (which sounds like He will figure out a way to use you with all of your warts), but you were the one He *chose* to use. You won the pageant! You got the roses! The trophy awaits you! You are not second string, nor the last one available. You were His choice for this flight. He chose you. It is a wonderful thing to finally know and truly believe.

It seems we have offered a lot of checkpoints and directives concerning this phase of the instruction of the arrow. This leads me to believe that the Lord has a lot to say about the selection process. Still, if you will allow, I want to offer just a few more possible insights. After all, you would not have picked up this book if you were not looking for confirmation in some areas of your life. Search the list below, asking The Archer to give you specific answers as you make your way from question to question. Take this time to allow Him to search a little deeper, revealing your heart and your positioning. For example; instead of simply reading "You sense His hovering presence," take a moment and look deep, and ask the Father, "Do I feel Your presence around me? Oh, Father, I pray that I would be more aware of Your constant watch care and Your hovering presence. Open my eyes to see, my ears to hear, and my heart to understand that You are everywhere, at all times." Take what is not actually interactive, and make it a very special time of reflection between you and the Father.

Have you been chosen for flight?

> You sense His hovering presence.
> The inner searching has become intense.
> Small moral compromises that were not issues before, have now become convictions.
> Living a Holy life has become important.
> You find yourself digging in to scriptures you once skimmed over and assumed you knew.
> The small flaws are no longer hidden.
> You are fully aware of all that would prevent you from striking the mark.
> You are not condemned, but convicted and called to a higher standard.
> His Holiness has become a glaring backdrop against which your rebellious nature is displayed.

Any of this sound familiar? I would dare say it probably has your name all over it.

Be encouraged, beloved, you are in the palm of His hand. His gaze is fixed upon you. What a wonderful place to be! With the revelation of your position, comes the revelation of His.

Can I get an *Ahhhh, Jesus!*?

He is bigger, holier, greater, purer – and you have just been covered and surrounded by all that He is. Chosen, you have become a weapon in His hand.

Oh, teachable arrow, if this is where you are - rejoice! Savor the moment. Flawed, yet favored, your life is about to change. You are getting ready to head into one of the most amazing seasons of your life.

Will it be easy? Absolutely not.

Will it be worth it? You better believe it!

You, my friend, are getting ready for the test of trueness. Ah, and you just may find yourself enjoying that which once frightened you - short term test flights.

Tested for True

But he knows where I am and what I've done. He can cross-examine me all he wants, and I'll pass the test with honors. I've followed him closely, my feet in his footprints, not once swerving from his way.

Job 23:10

I think at one time or another, each of us has had the wonderful experience of being chosen to participate in a ballgame of some sort. I personally really enjoyed softball. I played third base on my high school girl's team. This was back when I still went out in public in shorts with baseball imprints on my shins.

The Coalfield Yellow Jackets (impressive, huh?), could smack a baseball around. We had a lot of fun, and a lot of attitude. We practiced faithfully. We did not have the best equipment, but we knew how to utilize what we had. Our greatest asset, however, was our ability to intimidate the other team with trash talk. Not the profane type, the mess-with-your-mind sort.

Bet you thought you were gonna hit that didn't you?
Man, that was just purely painful to watch, embarrassing even for me... and I'm just playin' third base.
What happened to the A string? Are they playing on another field?

Is your dad the coach or something?
No offense, I'm just tryin' to make sense of why you're actually on this field.
But I'm sure you're good at something. Just because you stink at baseball doesn't mean you're a total loser.

Okay, I admit, it wasn't nice. I was a little competitive back then. But the point was to unnerve the opposition; distract them with meaningless chatter so they could not pick up the signals being sent out by the coach. The added benefit was that anger and frustration kept them from being fully focused on what they were supposed to be doing.

Distraction 101. It's a basic tactic in all games where focus is crucial. Granted, it usually only worked for a short period of time. But, for that short period of time, I had a lot of fun. After that, they grew accustomed to my tactics and were able to avoid the pitfalls of becoming frustrated with me. In essence, they learned (through repetition) how to deal with opposition and keep their eye on the prize. Only when they learned this were they able to move beyond us and take on the bigger dogs.

Why am I telling you this? Because this is where you are in the process. You are getting ready to be trained by some resistance and opposition, and (more than likely) some meaningless chatter. Some things may be thrown at you during this phase that require you to keep your mind stayed on Him with greater consistency. You are getting ready to be asked to maintain focus and ignore distraction, so that you may move on. Only when you get beyond this testing of steadfast focus and attentive obedience will you advance and move forward in the process.

It is during this time (Tested for True) that The Archer is watching to see if the arrow will fly true, or become distracted in flight. It is during this time that The Archer watches the bend and tendencies of the arrow.

One thing Hal does in the testing is to hold the arrow in the center of his palm and spin it. It reveals the bend, or any deviation in weight of center. For some reason, this just makes me laugh. I don't know about you, but there have most definitely been times in my life when I felt like a spun puppy. The thing is, I usually rebuked the enemy, when in fact it was a turn of The Archer's hand that sent me reeling. He was checking my balance.

Oh, we could just camp here for a while. How many of us struggle when our routine changes, or someone throws us a curve? When trial, offense, distraction, or temptation hit, how long does it take us to regain focus and find center, and get steady on our feet again?

Think for just a moment about the last time you thought you were being attacked, when in fact you were being tested. Did you rebuke, when in fact you should have thanked God and found your focal point again? What did you learn?

I have found that true revelation comes in the spin. It is in these moments that we see how easily we can refocus and get back into proper alignment. It sounds a bit simplistic, but God truly wants us to be able to find our way home after spinning out. He teaches us to do just that.

> *Anyone who meets a testing challenge head-on and manages to stick it out is mighty fortunate. For such persons loyally in love with God, the reward is life and more life.*

Don't let anyone under pressure to give in to evil say, "God is trying to trip me up." God is impervious to evil, and puts evil in no one's way. The temptation to give in to evil comes from us and only us. We have no one to blame but the leering, seducing flare-up of our own lust. Lust gets pregnant, and has a baby: sin! Sin grows up to adulthood, and becomes a real killer. So, my very dear friends, don't get thrown off course. Every desirable and beneficial gift comes out of heaven. The gifts are rivers of light cascading down from the Father of Light. There is nothing deceitful in God, nothing two-faced, nothing fickle. He brought us to life using the true Word, showing us off as the crown of all his creatures.

Post this at all the intersections, dear friends: Lead with your ears, follow up with your tongue, and let anger straggle along in the rear. God's righteousness doesn't grow from human anger. So throw all spoiled virtue and cancerous evil in the garbage. In simple humility, let our gardener, God, landscape you with the Word, making a salvation-garden of your life. Don't fool yourself into thinking that you are a listener when you are anything but, letting the Word go in one ear and out the other. Act on what you hear! Those who hear and don't act are like those who glance in the mirror, walk away, and two minutes later have no idea who they are, what they look like.

But whoever catches a glimpse of the revealed counsel of God - the free life! - even out of the corner of his eye, and sticks with it, is no distracted scatterbrain but a man or woman of action. That person will find delight and affirmation in the action.

James 1:12-25

Did you catch the three directives given in the beginning of verse 19? Let me share it with you from the NIV:

> *My dear brothers, take note of this: Everyone should be quick to listen, slow to speak and slow to become angry...*
>
> James 1:19 (NIV)

Quick to listen.
Slow to speak.
Slow to anger.

Oh guys, if we could just get this, it would change so much! So many of us have the order reversed. We are quick to speak and rash in our anger. We do not listen, I mean really listen, because all too often we really do not care what anyone else has to say. It is our own opinions we value and consider most important, not the counsel of those with whom God has surrounded us. In fact, if their opinions differ, we feel a great need to convince them of their folly and bring them around to our way of thinking. Isn't that nuts? Most of the time we are not even fully convinced of our own "rightness," but we still want/need everyone to agree with us.

Remember: Quick to listen, slow to speak, slow to anger... and quick to find our focal point while walking sideways out of a spin. Can we all just go there? Can we pass the hand-spun test?

When an arrow has passed my husband's initial examination and has been chosen, he puts it to the real test. Yes, we all know that only one test will prove the trueness of an arrow.

It must fly.

An archer does not know if an arrow is completely true until it strikes the mark it has been released to strike. In keeping with this, Hal takes the chosen arrows and sends them on short flights. He will test an arrow several times before determining its trueness. How foolish it would be to go into competition - or more importantly, battle - with an untried arrow. When the mark demands a precision strike, an arrow with even the slightest bend is going to miss. The effect of pressure, distance and speed on a slight bend is enormous in the final outcome. Small deviations over time become huge directional divisions.

Deviate: *to stray, especially from a standard or principle.*

Listen to the Spirit my brothers and sisters. Those small bends and tiny distraction can lead you so far off course over time that you no longer recognize your surroundings. You can find yourself wondering how in the world you got all the way out into the middle of this wilderness.

You see, the enemy rarely uses huge things to move us; otherwise we might become wise to his tactics. The small deviations are much less noticeable, and when joined with a bit of time, are all the enemy needs to bind you to a distant tree and leave you longing for the straight path.

Perhaps in the natural world, an arrow striking or missing the mark could have to do with the skill of the archer. A true arrow could miss the target when sent by an unskilled archer. But you and I both know that is not the case with The Master Archer. *God does not miss.* Any variance from center is found in the arrow, not The Archer.

Can I get an amen?

I do not know about you, but I have most definitely missed some of the marks I was supposed to strike; and it was without a doubt, my fault. Most of my missed marks had everything to do with what we just touched upon - distraction and small deviations from course. I would be sent from the hand of The Archer with a specific target in sight; only to lose focus as those around me caught my attention. Distraction comes in many forms. Praise, recognition, rebuke, ridicule, disapproval, approval. Both pretty things and scary monsters serve the same purpose: to distract. All can take your eyes off of the mark.

> *Keep vigilant watch over your heart; that's where life starts. Don't talk out of both sides of your mouth; avoid careless banter, white lies, and gossip. Keep your eyes straight ahead; ignore all sideshow distractions. Watch your step, and the road will stretch out smooth before you. Look neither right nor left; leave evil in the dust.*
>
> Proverbs 4:23

> *I'm on my way; I'll be there soon. Keep a tight grip on what you have so no one distracts you and steals your crown.*
>
> Revelation 3:11

The Master Archer has one thing on His mind during this time of testing for true: Will they go where I tell them to go, and do what I tell them to do?

My husband is a skilled archer. He knows if the arrow goes flying off to the left, it must be straightened and shaped toward the right. If it flies to the right, adjustments must be made to the left. He can watch the arrow fly and know what needs to be tweaked or improved upon.

God, The Archer, does the same. He sends us on these short flights and watches in what direction we might be bent. He knows if our tendency is to move *this* way, He must mold us *that* way. He is not scrutinizing the flight so that He may shake His head in disgust and shatter the arrow over His knee. He is watching the flight so that He might make a more precision instrument.

You see, the speed at which an arrow flies negates any possible mid-flight adjustments. The arrow must be straight, fully aligned; only then will it obey the slightest touch of The Archer. When an arrow has truly been adjusted and bent by a Master Archer, He knows that wherever He sends it, it is going to strike dead center - no fluctuation, and no deviation from course. Archers will not use an arrow that they cannot trust to fly true. I suppose they may use it for practice and for non-specific missions, but never for those life and death flights; the ones where eternity shifts. Only a tested, true arrow receives that kind of assignment.

Faithfulness and steadfastness are crucial during this phase of the process. You may not always like the destination of your short flights, but do not fight the aim of The Archer. You might think that another arrow would be more suited for this menial flight, but do not refuse the mission. Every flight is for your training; every mark struck, a breath of proven trust in the lungs of The Archer.

Do you realize how precious these "small" and "mundane" journeys are? Small is not small in the Kingdom, and the mundane is quite significant in unseen realms. These are the profound and precious moments when your life revolves around pleasing Him; your greatest delight coming from serving in absolute surrender, waiting upon Him.

> *They threw their crowns at the foot of the Throne, chanting, Worthy, O Master! Yes, our God! Take the glory! The honor! The power! You created it all;*
>
> Revelation 4:9

Friend, this is a time even sweeter than the moments in His hand; for these are the days when you place offerings at the feet of your Beloved. Crowns of obedience, faithfulness, humility, quiet strength, determination, complete focus and fealty are won during these days, and your greatest pleasure becomes the opportunity to return to the hand of The Archer having accomplished all He has sent you to accomplish.

When Jesus Christ becomes Lord of our lives, we begin a journey that should one day exchange our selfish nature for His generous nature. Where we once loved to get, we now long to give; our greatest pleasure coming from sharing, pouring and releasing. Ah, and giving to Him, lavishing our love on Him - there is nothing to compare with the joy it brings.

The motivation of the arrow changes and the arrow flies from the heart of truth with the sole intent of striking the mark in order to lay the victory at the feet of The Archer. What an honor to give back (in even the smallest measure) to the One Who has given so much!

An interesting thing about an arrow; it has no say in where it is sent. Though we would like to think otherwise, in all of my years watching Hal practice his craft, not once have I heard an arrow talk back to him, or observed it holding onto the bow, refusing release.

Unfortunately, the same cannot be said of the human arrow. We have opinions and consider it an absolute right and responsibility to voice them on a regular basis. We catch a glimpse of one of our test flights and we argue until we are blue in the face.

My gifts do not line up with this destination! I am quite sure that I was designed to strike a golden mark. I mean, where's the microphone? I am called to a pulpit, a podium and a pedestal. I am no ordinary arrow!

We see ourselves aiming straight for a behind-the-scenes-not-so-glamorous bull's-eye and as the mop and broom fill our line of vision, we make a quick left. *I rebuke you Satan! Gettest thouests hands off of God's anointed!* We run back to The Archer and try to thrust ourselves upon the bow for a re-shoot. Wiping our brows, we turn to The Archer and look at Him as if to say, *did you see what almost happened to me?*

Let's try this again. The Archer pulls back the arrow for another test flight. The relief of another destination permeates the arrow, right before it plunges into a bucket full of soapy water with a sponge.

Moral: You will not receive another assignment until you complete the first with faithfulness.

Please understand, you are not being tested for true when you send yourself on the trips you would like to take. This is not about taking in the sights and showing everyone your feathers in flight. This is a test of obedience. If you are not obedient, you do not pass. Pretty basic.

You see, The Archer does not grade on the curve, nor does He compare one arrow to another (Thank you, Jesus!). He simply gives the assignment. Some complete the homework; some do not. Those that do not are not rejected, but are set aside for a time of reshaping and remolding. These arrows will be given other opportunities to fly, and they will choose (by levels of faithfulness) the degree of flight importance.

These arrows (if pliable in His hand) will get another opportunity to be tested for true.

With your very own hands you formed me; now breathe your wisdom over me so I can understand you. When they see me waiting, expecting your Word, those who fear you will take heart and be glad. I can see now, God, that your decisions are right; your testing has taught me what's true and right.

Psalm 119:73

The small flights are teacher flights. If we refuse the small, we will not see the great. Some of us need to absolutely jump at the chance to do the small; the opportunity to minister in the hidden positions. Our pride keeps us from volunteering for the menial. We have convinced ourselves that we were made for "grander stuff." While I understand that pull and that mentality, even that particular bend of teaching, I can tell you that the grand is birthed through the small. Just ask an oak tree.

Have you come to the place in your life where you can look at the challenges as sheer gifts? Do you fully understand that it is when you are under pressure that your true colors show brightest? Do you know that God is watching the display? Is your display for you, or for Him? Are you content to stay in the process no matter how long it takes, or do you get frustrated because God is not acting quickly enough for you?

These are all tests of trueness.

I would imagine at this point you might want to throw this book against the wall and throw yourself one of those pity parties we talked about in the introduction. I mean, how can any of us ever hope to be good enough to test true? It's very simple, actually.

He is a merciful Archer.

> *He forgives your sins – every one.*
> *He heals your diseases – every one.*
> *He redeems you from hell – saves your life!*
> *He crowns you with love and mercy – a paradise crown.*
> *He wraps you in goodness – beauty eternal.*
> *He renews your youth – you're always young in his presence.*
> *God makes everything come out right;*
> *he puts victims back on their feet.*
> *He showed Moses how he went about his work,*
> *opened up his plans to all Israel.*
> *God is sheer mercy and grace;*
> *not easily angered, he's rich in love.*
> *He doesn't endlessly nag and scold,*
> *nor hold grudges forever.*
> *He doesn't treat us as our sins deserve,*
> *nor pay us back in full for our wrongs.*
> *As high as heaven is over the earth,*
> *so strong is his love to those who fear him.*
> *And as far as sunrise is from sunset,*
> *he has separated us from our sins.*
> *As parents feel for their children,*
> *God feels for those who fear him.*
> *He knows us inside and out,*
> *keeps in mind that we're made of mud...*

Psalm 103:3-18

As we walk through this phase of the arrows instruction, be ever mindful of God's grace. Remember that test flights are monitored by the God Who "keeps in mind that we're made of mud." That should keep us from getting haughty, huh? (So, I guess if we were made of mud, it was not so unusual for Jesus to spit in the dirt and form mud balls for the eyes of the blind man... it was a simple graft of original material.)

Once again a bunny trail.

You have been chosen and tested for true. A bit ruffled in feather, yet keener in focus, you have proven faithful. The Archer knows He can trust you to fly straight. What a glorious moment! What great hope surges through you, for you have been chosen and proven true. You are learning things about yourself that drop you to your knees, and learning things about Him that bring you to your feet again.

How great is this Archer God?

You know you have been walking through this stage of the process if:

> You think you know where you are headed, but...you are wrong.
> You have been in a time of intimate relationship with Christ; only to feel like that closeness is being tested.
> Distractions surround you on every side.
> You feel like you have banged into a few spiritual walls.
> Your first instinct is to run back to His hand.
> You experience tremendous joy when you sense His pleasure.
> You find yourself looking for opportunities to make God smile.
> You have an increased awareness of the seriousness of your flight on this planet.
> You long for crowns to place at His feet.

Now what? How do you move into the next phase? You get obedient in even the smallest of spirit-urgings. Anything the Father instructs you to do; do it! Not only that, but move willingly and joyfully into all areas of service into which He might lead you. For, you see, the truest purpose of the arrow is the fulfillment of the will of The Archer. An arrow is selfless. An arrow performs by the hand of The Archer alone. The sooner the arrow comes to that knowledge, the sooner the arrow steps into the next phase.

Here's the kicker. You would think if an arrow has been tested for true and flies straight on short assignments, the next phase would be a longer flight. Ah, but the next phase makes you long for even the shortest of journeys, for the next phase does not put you in flight, but into a hidden position.

How could that possibly make sense? Everything within us begins to raise the voice of protest: *But, you see, Master Archer, I'm a flier!*

His response: *Not until I say you are, Little Arrow.*

Hidden

Don't you see that children are God's best gift? The fruit of the womb his generous legacy? Like a warrior's fistful of arrows are the children of a vigorous youth. Oh, how blessed are you parents, with your quivers full of children! Your enemies don't stand a chance against you; you'll sweep them right off your doorstep.

Psalm 127:3

Sharpen the arrows! Fill the quivers!

Jeremiah 51:11

Positioned, chosen, tested for true, you have come through with flying colors (no pun intended). The urgency inside of you feels like it has reached a fevered pitch. With every single move of His hand, you jump and respond. You are quickened and very keen in the spirit. You have known His upward call in your spirit, experienced the warm intimacy of His hand, and remained faithful and true in times of testing. You have a great sense of expectancy, and a deep longing to fly beyond where you are at this moment. In fact, you are so ready you can't see straight. Fully convinced that your glory moment is just around the corner, the word *Tada!* and the throwing open of hands are restrained just beneath the surface. Your spirit feels like a kid who drank too much red

Kool-Aid. You are ready to bounce off of all of the spiritual walls.

Like a vacationing child in the back seat, the *are we there yet's?* have overtaken all other thought and conversation. *Can I fly now?* No. *Can I fly now?* No. *What about now?* No. *Is now better?* No. *Are you sure now is not good?* Yes. *Did you say yes, I could fly now?* No.

Restless, your feet hang out the window in anticipation, as you watch the clouds sweep by through the back window, seeming to mock your immobility.

I know some of you are here. In fact, I have seen your feet dangling and that faraway look in your eyes. You are full, confident, humbled and beautifully trained to strike the mark. You long for the feel of wind and the call to foreign lands. You have settled your issues and know He has called you. You have no doubt it is time to become the deadly weapon you know God has called you to be in the kingdom. The Kool-Aid surging through your veins, you sense in the deepest part of you that God is getting ready to divinely position you.

You are absolutely right.

Welcome to the quiver.

Ah, the quiver. This is where all true arrows find themselves from time to time. No, we do not long for the quiver. We long to streak across the sky like the beautiful things we know we are, but just as our toes touch sunlight, we are planted snugly in the middle of the other arrows. There is most definitely some kind of mistake here. Crowded, bumped, jostled and feeling suddenly ordinary, we look around with a bit of incredulous disdain.

What in the world just happened? We do what any arrow with limited vision does: *I rebuke you Satan! Take your hands off of God's anointed! I am called to nations!*

But the hand that just fit you closely to the other arrows felt disconcertingly familiar; like the hand that held you closely and lovingly during the choosing process. From somewhere deep within, you hear His words, "Love deeply…"

> *Love from the center of who you are; don't fake it. Run for*
> *dear life from evil; hold on for dear life to good. Be good*
> *friends who love deeply; practice playing second fiddle.*
>
> Romans 12:9-10

Our inner conversations begin: *What do you mean practice playing second fiddle? Man! This stinks. I went through all that I have gone through* (violins please…); *the frustrated pull, the patient longing, the close scrutiny, the test flights, realigning, shaping, molding, training and have proven I will fly true… for this? I am way beyond this place spiritually, Lord. These arrows you stuck me with just don't get it. They cannot fly like I fly. In fact, they are limiting my progress in you… holding me back.*

Any archer worth their salt will tell you that a whiny arrow is a flawed arrow, one on the verge of cracking. There is no power in a whiny arrow. So, as you whine, keep in mind that this is exactly why you are in the quiver. Griping, complaining, whining, bad attitude, rebellion, resistance, shut down, melt down, apathy, complacency, laziness, discontent, sloth - these will make you a resident of the quiver for years on end. Just ask that little group that wandered around the desert for forty years. Big, bad, hot, dusty quiver.

Caleb's testimony is a perfect example of God-imposed quiver time. He *got it*, yet was still required to stay with the other arrows. Though he longed for flight, he wanted the others to fly with him.

Let's take a small flight through his life.

> *But my servant Caleb – this is a different story. He has a different spirit; he follows me passionately. I'll bring him into the land that he scouted and his children will inherit it.*

Numbers 14:24

> *The LORD said to Moses, "Send some men to explore the land of Canaan, which I am giving to the Israelites. From each ancestral tribe send one of its leaders." So at the LORD's command Moses sent them out from the Desert of Paran. All of them were leaders of the Israelites...*
> *"See what the land is like and whether the people who live there are strong or weak, few or many. What kind of land do they live in? Is it good or bad? What kind of towns do they live in? Are they unwalled or fortified? How is the soil? Is it fertile or poor? Are there trees on it or not? Do your best to bring back some of the fruit of the land." (It was the season for the first ripe grapes.) So they went up and explored the land...*
> *They came back to Moses and Aaron and the whole Israelite community at Kadesh in the Desert of Paran. There they reported to them and to the whole assembly and showed them the fruit of the land. They gave Moses this account: "We went into the land to which you sent us, and it does flow with milk and honey! Here is its fruit. But the people who live there are powerful, and the cities are fortified and very large. We even saw descendants of Anak*

there. The Amalekites live in the Negev; the Hittites, Jebusites and Amorites live in the hill country; and the Canaanites live near the sea and along the Jordan."

Then Caleb silenced the people before Moses and said, "We should go up and take possession of the land, for we can certainly do it." But the men who had gone up with him said, "We can't attack those people; they are stronger than we are." And they spread among the Israelites a bad report about the land they had explored. They said, "The land we explored devours those living in it. All the people we saw there are of great size. We saw the Nephilim there (the descendants of Anak come from the Nephilim). We seemed like grasshoppers in our own eyes, and we looked the same to them."

Numbers 13:1-3, 18-21, 26-33 (NIV)

Yes, Caleb *got it*. He was ready, willing and able to head into the promise, just as you feel you are, at this point. But God did not release him from the quiver. He had to stay with the other arrows and lead them. You see, just because you have grabbed hold of the vision (and even gone through some intensive training), does not mean you are getting ready to be sent into the middle of your destined strike point. Sometimes, you must stay in the quiver with the other arrows until they are ready to be sent as well.

For, you see, the greater purpose is an all out occupation, not a small incursion.

Moses, Aaron, Joshua and Caleb all knew what God had told them. They knew they could take the land because God said so. Still, when they presented the case to the people, even begging them to see what God could do, the others just couldn't go there with them. But the key is in what Moses did when the others failed to catch the vision. He interceded for them before God.

Can you even begin to imagine what would happen to the Body of Christ if His people began to truly intercede for those who had no vision? What about those who frustrate or aggravate us? What if intercession (birthed of sincere love) were our first response instead of our last resort? Ah, my huggable arrows, Kingdoms would tremble!

If we found true contentment and passion in every stage of our instruction, we might all have walls tumbling. That is what happens when God's people become committed to the process of steadfast, obedient, selfless love.

Though most do not like to hear it, Caleb stayed with the other arrows, even when his heart was fully convinced he could fly. He stayed because he knew God had him there for a reason. He was obedient not only in act, but in attitude of spirit.

Matthew Henry's Commentary describes Caleb in this way:

> "...he had another spirit, different from the rest of the spies, an after-spirit, which furnished him with second thoughts, and he followed the Lord fully, kept close to his duty, and went through with it, though deserted and threatened."

Now, pay attention to how he walked it out; for this is imperative to coming out of the time in the quiver: Caleb lived among the arrows that did not get it...

> "without dividing, – uprightly, without dissembling, – cheerfully, without disputing, – and constantly, without declining; and this is following him fully. Those that would follow God fully must have another spirit, another from the spirit of the world, and another from what their

own spirit has been. They must have the spirit of Caleb. Those that follow God fully in times of general apostasy God will own and honour by singular preservations in times of general calamity..."

What is your responsibility to the other arrows? What if you have the faith to move forward and the rest want to stay where they are? What if you are the only one who really believes you can take the land? Well, the answer we would like is to simply leave them behind, and let them find their own way. But, that just may be the wrong answer.

Sometimes, God's nature in us demands that we wait with those who cannot see, and pray that their eyes would be opened. It is not always God's way to send you flying from the quiver ahead of the others. He may let you carry the vision and spread it among the arrows, know the truth and walk it in their midst, and encourage them until they are truly ready to fly.

I know it is hard. You want to fly. You want to taste the wind, but God sometimes has you carry the vision in the close confines of the quiver, asking you to persevere and breathe life through the quiver, in hopes that the wind will find the faces of the others.

Can you love them that much? Can you forsake your desire in order to see someone else fulfill theirs? Can you be that selfless? Yes, it can be a painful place to walk. But when you enter that land you so long for, wouldn't it be wonderful to look beside you and see your brothers and sisters walking alongside? Wouldn't that be something? Instead of running ahead, wouldn't it be marvelous to enter in together?

Let me make this extremely simple for you by telling you something so profound it is elementary: The sole purpose of the quiver is to teach the arrow that love is the only reason to fly.

Your time on this planet is not about the love you receive, but about the love you give. It is not about how you are impacted by those around you, but how your life impacts theirs. Your journey is not one of collecting, but dispensing the love of God. The moment it becomes about what you can get, you have left the path. God has placed us on the earth to be givers; to implement His will in the earth, by loving and serving as He loved and served.

Oh, my friend, we come from a long and rich lineage of towel carrying feet washers - and there is no higher calling. How very like the enemy to make us a nation of consumers, when we were intended to be the ones who carried the supply for others.

There is this mindset in the Christian cosmos that says, *"Better is one day in your courts... and I'm never coming out."* We get full, satiated, and resplendent with what we think is God stuff and begin holding on for dear life. *Mine! More of God - all for me!* Then we take what we think He has given us and carve out nice comfy niche's we call positions, and settle in for years on end drinking from the one spiritual well we dug in the 70's. We slosh with stagnant waters, thanking God for our fullness, while others dehydrate and starve. But darlin', if the stuff you have can be hoarded and held back, it ain't God stuff. (Just had to use the word *ain't* there... it felt too right to this southern girl.)

God is a giver: Always has been, always will be. Everything about Him is extravagant. He holds nothing back, and if we have truly tapped into the stuff of God we cannot help but pour it out.

Life in the quiver (congregation) determines whether your desire to fly comes from selfish motive. We lose a lot of fliers here. Arrows that long to fly for their own glory, based on gifts alone, find it extremely difficult to stay in the quiver. In fact, if they are kept in the quiver for too long – forced to stay amidst the congregation - they will eventually blame the pastors and leaders for not seeing and acknowledging their gifts. They leave in search of a more "enlightened" group that can use them as they believe they are supposed to be used. Their hearts have been revealed. A refusal to love and submit in body life shows a lack of readiness for flight. Those that do not love have not learned the lesson of the quiver.

Can I tell you that this is a huge issue in the body of Christ; frustrated people jumping from church to church looking for someone who will put a microphone in their hands or a title on their door?

Why do we do that? Why do we want to go into "the ministry" when we do not even like the people that much? We have no heart to be amidst the other arrows.

> *If anyone boasts, "I love God," and goes right on hating his brother or sister, thinking nothing of it, he is a liar. If he won't love the person he can see, how can he love the God he can't see? The command we have from Christ is blunt: Loving God includes loving people. You've got to love both.*
> 1 John 4:20-21

Hear my heart, beloved; the only thing that bridges the gap between the pulpit and the people is love. Everything else is just chatter - sounding brass and clanging cymbal.

Time hidden away in the quiver is when the arrow's heart is most clearly displayed. Your interaction with others, or the lack thereof, is very telling. In the quiver, time becomes quite revelatory. With its passing, you will move into deeper levels of love and acceptance or you will be rendered immobile by selfish ambition. Will you long to leave the others in your search for flight, or will your deepest desire be to watch them fly? Your motives glow neon in the quiver. You see them, I see them, we all see them. But most importantly, God sees them… and your flight is either scheduled or delayed.

The most frequent complaint I hear as a leader is, "they just don't get it." Behind that sentence I usually hear how much further someone has advanced in their walk with God than the others in the body. It is a comment which searches for my permission to abandon post and look for a more "spiritually aggressive" group to hang with. They want me to tell them to enter Canaan alone and leave the others behind.

I have now come to the place where I simply tell them what I have found to be true in so many lives; I tell them they will hit the same wall wherever they go. For you see, walls are what you find when seeking feelings, signs and wonders, while God is trying to birth a love for His people in the depths of your soul.

Let me be as direct as I know how, because this is where many arrows disappear never to be seen again. Plainly put, if you resent your time in the quiver (with the people/congregation) and refuse to learn to love, you can spend the rest of your life in this place. Though you were created for more, God will absolutely leave you hidden until you get this. Love, deep and abiding love, is that which will place you back in The Archer's hand as if drawn by magnetic force.

Mark this, dear arrow, once firmly ensconced within the quiver only two things can bring you out: love or open rebellion. One delivers and one binds up. Please hear me. It does not matter how many churches you try, what groups you attend, or how many times someone lays hands on you and tells you how anointed you are - if you have no love for the other arrows, God will not use you. He will not use you because He cannot trust you to be good to His people. If He cannot trust your love for them, He will never place you in a position where you might bring them harm. That is truly the bottom line.

Though it has become so familiar we rarely plumb its richer depths, I present to you God's plan for deliverance from the quiver:

> *If I speak with human eloquence and angelic ecstasy but don't love, I'm nothing but the creaking of a rusty gate. If I speak God's Word with power, revealing all his mysteries and making everything plain as day, and if I have faith that says to a mountain, "Jump," and it jumps, but I don't love, I'm nothing. If I give everything I own to the poor and even go to the stake to be burned as a martyr, but I don't love, I've gotten nowhere. So, no matter what I say, what I believe, and what I do, I'm bankrupt without love. Love never gives up. Love cares more for others than for self. Love doesn't want what it doesn't have. Love doesn't strut, Doesn't have a swelled head, Doesn't force itself on others, Isn't always "me first," Doesn't fly off the handle, Doesn't keep score of the sins of others, Doesn't revel when others grovel, Takes pleasure in the flowering of truth, Puts*

54

up with anything, Trusts God always, Always looks for the best, Never looks back, But keeps going to the end.

Love never dies. Inspired speech will be over some day; praying in tongues will end; understanding will reach its limit. We know only a portion of the truth, and what we say about God is always incomplete. But when the Complete arrives, our incompletes will be canceled. When I was an infant at my mother's breast, I gurgled and cooed like any infant. When I grew up, I left those infant ways for good. We don't yet see things clearly. We're squinting in a fog, peering through a mist. But it won't be long before the weather clears and the sun shines bright! We'll see it all then, see it all as clearly as God sees us, knowing him directly just as he knows us!

But for right now, until that completeness, we have three things to do to lead us toward that consummation: Trust steadily in God, hope unswervingly, love extravagantly. And the best of the three is love.

1 Corinthians 13

This kind of love is what we must learn to walk out in the quiver. This is where everything finally takes on a sense of true purpose. This is a place of deep God-wisdom, and here, my friend, is where the arrow finally receives its razor edge, becoming a lethal weapon in the hand of The Archer.

As iron sharpens iron, so one man sharpens another.

Proverbs 27:17 (NIV)

This is where the arrow finally has a point. Love must become the point.

Take just a few minutes and consider the following questions. Ponder a few things in your heart and answer them in the privacy of your own mind. Let them become personal checkpoints.

If I asked you how you felt about the Body of Christ, what would be your truest response?

Are you involved in the lives of those in your local body?

What are your involvements?

Has your local body become a "family" to you?

If so, how do you purposely serve them?

Have you ever made yourself available to serve in whatever capacity you might be needed?

Does your service come with stipulations and contingencies?

Have you been guilty of grumbling among the arrows? When and why?

If so, have you repented of your bad attitude; turning away from it and moving in the opposite direction?

Have you seriously entertained the thought of leaving your church or group within the past three months, even though you know it was God Who brought you into it?

Becoming discontent with your spiritual positioning, coupled with a strong desire to change your physical positioning (out of frustration, not God-call) is a huge YOU ARE HERE sign. You can buy the t-shirt now. You are in the quiver.

Here, your two greatest tools are to love extravagantly and serve faithfully. Let me say that again: love extravagantly and serve faithfully. Pay attention to the adverbs – extravagant and faithful. Selflessness is the song that must be offered up during this phase of instruction.

You are probably in the quiver if:

> You are so frustrated with the other "arrows" you want to cry.
>
> You cannot see why "they" just don't get it.
>
> Spiritually, you think you have outgrown "them."
>
> You have the tendency to pick others apart and judge their walk.
>
> You just want to move beyond this place.
>
> You know you must be doing something wrong, but it is easier to blame the other arrows.
>
> You ask the Father what to do, and He repeatedly tells you to walk in love.
>
> You do not want to walk in love.
>
> You know you must, or you are never getting out of here.
>
> You catch glimpses of daylight and long to be sent flying.

Does this sound like you? Oh, bless your heart!

You have a couple of options here. You can despise the arrows, or bless them. Your choice will determine the length of your stay. But let me encourage you to love, dear one, for when you rest among the precious arrows, you are truly in the company of greatness.

Exposed

> *The purity of silver and gold is tested by putting them in the fire;*
> *The purity of human hearts is tested by giving them a little fame.*
>
> Proverbs 27:21

Sing with me as you click your ruby slippers together...

All we need is love... da da da da da ... all we need is love.

Whew! Bet you thought you were going to be stuck in that quiver forever, didn't you? Ah, but you were mistaken. You have places to go, things to do and marks to strike. I suddenly have this image of all these guys named *Mark* getting smacked around. (Sorry, it's just this mind God gave me.) It is time for the next stage in the preparation of an arrow.

Now that you have learned to get along with, and yes, even love the other arrows, a wonderful thing begins to take place: Where you once sought the opening of the quiver so that you might make your escape, you now long for the opening so that your newfound friends might take their own flight. You once longed for your own open door, but you now long for the door to open for others. At least, that is what is supposed to happen.

Life in the quiver (in the midst of the congregation), when spent breathing the breath of The Archer, and feeling His heartbeat all around, should radically change the motivators, intentions and purposes of the arrow. God breath does that. His rhythm pounding through your veins makes you live your life in a different key, with greater resonance. Go figure.

When placed in the quiver, the arrow is already a mighty weapon. It has been chosen and tested as true. It longs for the battle, hungers for the target it is supposed to fly toward - its destiny, so to speak.

Gotta move into the destiny God has for me. Time for me to fly! Use me, God! Take me into Your hand, and send me on my way!

Ahhhhh! You can just hear the cry of the chosen arrow.

In the beginning of its time in the quiver, this arrow has prayed repeatedly for release; begged for daylight, whined incessantly and even tried to jump out. Blame and judgment has been cast on the other arrows and disdain for their "lesser enlightenment" has laced the days of the whiny arrow. Tears, "righteous" anger (clue: we are not that righteous), sniveling, and new quiver contemplation (*I want a new church…*) have held you back. But now, you have cried it all out, left snuffing and shoulders shaking behind and finally just wore yourself out.

Eyes puffy and nose bulbous, something unexpected happens; the other arrows surround you and begin to offer solace. Kindness, compassion and understanding begin to flow from the arrows that have known the quiver on repeated journeys. You begin to see that they are not so "unenlightened" as you thought, but that you, (yes, you!)

were the one who had some growing to do, some enlightenment to gain.

Revelation has come, and with it a love and respect for the others that you never knew you could possess. Big, strong, all-about-me arrow has become intricately entwined with the other arrows (Bliss!). They have become a unit, instead of lone rangers (I know... mixed euphemisms again). The cry has changed from "use me" to "use us!"

Major transition. Huge!

Not only that, the arrow is now trying to help the others find their place of usefulness. The arrow actually attempts to help others come into the hand of The Archer before taking its own journey, wanting others to fulfill their destiny first. The Arrow just came to life.

> *We know that we have passed from death to life, because we love our brothers.*
>
> 1 John 3:14 (NIV)

The destiny of the arrow just clarified. They get it. They see it. The light bulb flickers, then flames to brilliant life as the arrow finally understands; its destiny is beautifully interwoven with the others. Its greatest mission will be found in loving and caring for the others. Wiser and more humble, the arrow's order of all things significant, changes - others come before self, sending its small selfish world sliding off of the me-equator; bringing and birthing (dare I say it?) a new world order.

Get it? *Order of significance... selfish world... new world order...* Hah! Never thought I would find a reason to use that phrase.

The world of the arrow, and the order of the arrow has become new, and the one most surprised by the massive change? You guessed it; the little arrow. You just didn't see love being the deeper answer, did you?

> *If you've gotten anything at all out of following Christ, if his love has made any difference in your life, if being in a community of the Spirit means anything to you, if you have a heart, if you care – then do me a favor: Agree with each other, love each other, be deep-spirited friends. Don't push your way to the front; don't sweet-talk your way to the top. Put yourself aside, and help others get ahead. Don't be obsessed with getting your own advantage. Forget yourselves long enough to lend a helping hand.*
>
> Philippians 2:1-4

What? How'd that happen? Can you say, *QuiverTime*? *Na Na Na Na can't touch this…* Oh my goodness! Somebody needs a little sleep.

Friend, time spent among the other arrows, hidden in the quiver, teaches us to love and to serve. As much as we would like a different answer, it is what it is. There is nothing deeper; no formula that will bypass this part of the equation. Love delivers. Service follows. You can serve without love, but you cannot love without serving. Period. We all know what the Word says about this, don't we?

> *When the other ten heard of this conversation, they lost their tempers with James and John. Jesus got them together to settle things down. "You've observed how godless rulers throw their weight around," he said, "and when people get a little power how quickly it goes to their heads. It's not going to be that way with you. Whoever wants to be great*

must become a servant. Whoever wants to be first among
you must be your slave. That is what the Son of Man has
done: He came to serve, not to be served – and then to give
away his life in exchange for many who are held hostage."

Mark 10:41-45

This is the true destiny of all arrows: to serve. You serve
wherever The Archer sends you. How do you serve? You
love, you cover, you encourage, you train, you teach, you
strengthen and you pray for all of those whom The Archer
brings into your sphere of influence. The Arrow serves the
will of The Archer. After all, an arrow has no purpose
without an archer. Revelation of love and service will
absolutely bring you out and up, and into His hand.

Ah, wise-arrows, having learned the lessons of the quiver, it
is time for something truly wondrous, something you have
been longing for - the feel of His hand as it surrounds you
and lifts you from your hidden place. Get ready to be
exposed; exposed to the elements, that is. Oh, and these are
elements unlike any you might have known up to this point,
as in one beautiful life-defining moment, The Archer
reaches deep into the quiver slung tight against His back and
His fingers lace around you. Oh, there is nothing like it! This
is a definite laughter-through-tears moment.

Having been hidden for some time now, it is a euphoric
feeling when you finally come into contact with the wind
again, the world taking on a hugeness you do not remember
it having before. Once self-centered and me-minded, it is
almost funny what has happened to you. You have become
so much a part of the group, finding deep love and
contentment in the quiver, you are actually surprised when
He singles you out and takes you firmly into His hand. Your

heart leaps, and you know a moment's fear as everything in you rises to the moment. Bright light, fierce winds, breath-taking ascent, the feel of His hand... pure bliss. This is joy time. Oh, how we need joy time! God brings you out from the midst and you find the indescribable pleasure of being chosen for a second time.

Just breathe!

This time, however, you exult in the choosing to a new and more profound degree, for you have grown and matured in the journey. Where your love for The Archer was once based on what He had done (and could do) for you, a deeper love, borne of time, trust and trial, has bloomed, and now demands a service response. You have developed a truer love, one birthed of quiet faith despite circumstance, and now, churning within you, is a hope unlike anything you have ever experienced.

You do not know why you are so full and so expectant. It isn't as if you could actually see the destination like this - coming up in position behind Him as you are (think arrow withdrawn from quiver and being pulled up over the shoulder). Ah, but you see Him in a profound and revelatory way. You sense Him in a surrounding, all-encompassing kind of way, and that is more than you dared dream before.

You do not have to see the destination, for you are fully and completely enveloped in the purpose of His hand. You are acutely aware of the mission and the call. It keeps you quickened and taut with strength as you move beyond the warm bosom of the quiver.

Who knew this existed? Who knew you could be called out, set apart and fly through the elements in the very hand of

God? Who knew you could be afraid, jubilant, peaceful and awestruck at the same time? Who knew you could be so quickened, so keen that the merest whisper of His breath could mark you and shake you to the core? Who would have ever dreamed it would feel like this to be brought out by His hand alone?

It most assuredly did not feel this way when you tried to bring yourself out all of those times before. Every time you tried to make something happen before, you were left empty and frustrated and feeling like you had failed in some way. After all, your attempt to deliver yourself just did not turn out as you would have liked. Ah, but this… this is His hand, and there is no doubt of the outcome. When He brings you out, darlin', He brings you out!

When you hit daylight you find that something unexpected and wonderful has happened in the close confines and constant friction of the quiver: You have been sharpened. You have become an instrument of war!

What? I thought I became soft in the quiver – the whole "love thing," you know.

But no, you find something unforeseen has again taken place. God's thoughts have once again been higher than yours, and what you thought He was doing, was in fact, far less than what was actually taking place (That's The Archer for you.). In becoming a servant, in loving the other arrows, and considering them before you considered yourself, you became stronger, sharper and keener than ever.

In becoming a servant, He made you a leader.

In birthing humility, He made you great.

Can we shout now? What kind of God does this?

Now you know the firm grip of His hand as He brings you to the highest point you have reached thus far. The other arrows cheer, and you know the rush of something heretofore unknown: destiny's deepest call. Your spirit trembles as His will becomes like blood pounding through your veins. Nothing in the flesh could ever prepare you for this moment; but He, yes, He has.

No longer hidden, knowing a great love for, but no longer feeling the restraint of the masses, your spirit fills with God-breath, and your eyes fill with tears of gratitude. You soar!

In practical, human-sight terms, these are the moments when God singles you out. Not for notoriety or fame - though at times, those things become by-products of God-flight. He singles you out for another kind of test, and this one is huge (and can find you right back in the quiver if failed). This test allows you to shine for glorious moments as He brings you out of hiding. This is the test in which you get noticed by the others. This test puts you somehow in front of those who might applaud or stand in awe of what you have accomplished in His hand. This test asks the question, *"If I let you fly beautifully, will you acknowledge The Archer or praise the Arrow?"*

In the temporal world, this phase might be evidenced by the taking on of a new position. Perhaps you are asked to teach, and you do it marvelously. You may be asked to step from the choir into a lead position on the worship team, and when you sing His presence absolutely fills the place. At work, you may be given new administrative assignments and in their implementation bring things into order and alignment, drawing *oohs* and *ahs* from those you serve. You have been waiting a long time for this opportunity to move, to shine, and it finally comes.

And God allows you to knock it out of the park.

Has this ever happened to you? Can you remember a time when God opened the door and brought you out big? You did not saunter in the back door, but parachuted into the front of the room. Through no planning or manipulation of your own, you have just been exposed. No longer hidden, you become the center of attention because He has let you reflect a bit of His glory - and everyone was quite impressed. You were so shiny!

Know this dear arrow: The Archer is wonderful at displaying the arrow to its best advantage. The question is will the arrow truly display The Archer?

Remember our opening verse?

> *The purity of silver and gold is tested by putting them in the fire; The purity of human hearts is tested by giving them a little fame.*
>
> Proverbs 27:21

If someone had mentioned this verse to me years ago, I might have made a few more effective flights. How about you?

Oh, guys, have I been there. The euphoria of being lifted out from the middle of the other arrows can most definitely go to your head. It is like holding your breath for months and then hyperventilating as you finally begin to breathe again. It's just so much, so fast! You are shiny, sharp and ready to fly. You hit the elements, the light begins to reflect off of you and you go suddenly stupid, thinking that you just might be the source of all of that radiant glory.

Just remember, you are merely a reflection, a mirror, a flash... never the source. Did I say *never*? My friend, the moment we even begin to think, *What a cool arrow I am!* ... the earth comes up to meet us fast! We fall mid-flight. Our prayer at that moment should not be *"Help me!"* but *"Father, please do not let me hurt anyone on my way down!"*

We see people in this phase all the time; then we scratch out heads and wonder where they went. A shiny arrow streaks across the sky drawing *oohs* and *ahs* - (Preachers, teachers, Levite's and kings) - and its song of praise begins to inexorably include the words *I, Me,* and *My*. What was once a melody born of thanksgiving and great humility becomes a clamorous and self-indulgent anthem when mingled with the empty platitudes of shallow watcher arrows.

Watcher arrows? You know who they are. They are the ones who applaud the flight, while ignoring The One Who made it happen. They adore the shine, serve the shine and seek the spiritual mirror-ball experience, never searching for the point from which it emanates. These are the religious groupies waiting on the sweat soaked towels and miniature oil bottles of the shiny arrows with the flashy feathers and microphones. (Oh, my goodness. Am I really going to leave that in this book? Guess so!)

Many true arrows cannot handle their opportunity to shine. Notice I did say *true* arrows. They have passed the initial tests, but those held no glory - and glory is the kicker. Glory can mess you up. The heart of man seeks a kind of glory that can never belong to him. Unrestrained, the search for glory destroys, and the longing to draw it unto oneself perverts and bends the good arrow. There is no grey area here, friend. All of the glory belongs to Him. It will never be yours. If you attempt to claim it, bask in it, borrow it or pervert it, you fall. Just ask Lucifer.

> *To him who is able to keep you from falling and to present you before his glorious presence without fault and with great joy - to the only God our Savior be glory, majesty, power and authority, through Jesus Christ our Lord, before all ages, now and forevermore! Amen.*
>
> Jude 1:24,25 (NIV)

What belongs to Him?

Glory
Majesty
Power
Authority

Glory: praise, honor, or distinction, beauty, splendor, great gratification or exaltation.

Majesty: sovereign power, greatness or splendor of quality or character.

Power: possession of control, or influence over other, ability to act or produce an effect.

Authority: power to influence or command thought, opinion, or behavior.

If they praise you, it is His. If you find honor, it belongs to Him. If you have any power, or walk in greatness, acknowledge Him. Any beauty you experience, any splendor you display, any gratification you receive, and all exaltation of any form - it all belongs to Him. If you wield any control or influence, produce any good effect, or command any generals, it is by His hand alone. Give it back, offer it up, pour it out and lavish it upon Him. Hold nothing back...

"...And He will keep you from falling..."

To some, the entire idea of hoarding praise and stealing glory seems so far from conceivable you have already decided to skim through this chapter. But please understand, I am not saying this is your weakness; I am saying if the enemy plays true to form, you will face this temptation in your flesh at some time. When you do, remember what I have said thus far.

Friend, though you have a right estimation of your gifts and abilities at this moment, esteem is a funny thing. Fed by God, it remains correctly balanced; fed by the enemy, it can become an unexpectedly boastful, pride-filled little devil. If angels can fall from heaven because of this issue, we would be quite foolish to think ourselves above it.

He replied, "I saw Satan fall like lightning from heaven..."

Luke 10:18 (NIV)

All your pomp has been brought down to the grave, along with the noise of your harps; maggots are spread out beneath you and worms cover you. How you have fallen from heaven, O morning star, son of the dawn! You have been cast down to the earth, you who once laid low the nations! You said in your heart, "I will ascend to heaven; I will raise my throne above the stars of God; I will sit enthroned on the mount of assembly, on the utmost heights of the sacred mountain. I will ascend above the tops of the clouds; I will make myself like the Most High."

Isaiah 14:11-14 (NIV)

Not a pretty picture. But then again, pride and arrogance never are. Let the wise take heed; pride and arrogance inevitably birth shame.

First pride, then the crash - the bigger the ego, the harder the fall.

Proverbs 16:18

Yes, the bigger the ego, the harder the fall. The result of pride and arrogance is shame; for pride is followed by falling and failure, and to the proud, a witnessed fall is filled with shame. And shame? Well, that is the very fingerprint of Satan. Shame should reveal his handiwork to you with great clarity.

Yes, a humble and healthy estimation of God's greatness and the profound privilege we walk in as His chosen is intrinsic to a successful season of exposure. In this, the sweetest of flights, you must continually be mindful of one core truth: You are the reflection - He is the source.

God is the only thing about you that has a forever shine. Everything else that looks good about you is smoke and mirrors. We all know what we really are when it comes right down to it. My shine rubs off pretty quickly. His never dulls, never diminishes and never fails to penetrate beyond human vision. His shine goes deep.

He deserves all glory and honor for every moment you spend in the light. Fellow arrow, heed well these words - you must never take the praise of men to heart. Do not let any portion of what belongs to The Archer become a notch upon the arrow. If you fly straight and strike your mark, it is because you have been sent by the skilled hand of the Master Archer.

As a simple warning, I must tell you, men have the uncanny ability to lift and promote you on their praises, and watcher arrows have a propensity for encouraging you to take flights they find most interesting. When you allow this to happen, you will never even come close to the mark you could have, and should have, struck with The Archer.

Let me explain for just a minute. A *few "Oh, you are just so good at thats!"* and *"You know, you really should justs…"* can send a faithful arrow flying toward a man-made flesh-feeder mark. Be awake, little children, multitudes of watcher arrows love to tell you how and where to fly, but are neither committed nor faithful enough to ever take those same flights themselves. They offer glory (and financial funding) to the reflection, praising all things that glitter, and in turn become bitter and accusatory when the reflection fades. It becomes their excuse for never flying; never advancing. They blame the reflection for not meeting their standard, and pour anger upon The Archer for their own distorted worship of lesser gods. Beware the praise of watcher arrows. All they want is shine and no substance.

How'd we get here? Back to topic.

Let's get really honest for a minute. Can you think of times when you took the glory that belonged to Him? Can you recall moments when you might have exulted in your accomplishments, patted your own back instead of acknowledging it was by His hand that you did it at all? If so, let's take just a moment and repent of a haughty or prideful attitude. Let's make sure that all praise and glory are lavished upon Him, where they belonged in the first place.

Now, there is a glory that is shared, but only because He allows us to share in it. It is like walking in His shadow - the shadow is still His, we just happen to be covered by it.

> *Now if we are children, then we are heirs - heirs of God and co-heirs with Christ, if indeed we share in his sufferings in order that we may also share in his glory.*
>
> Romans 8:17 (NIV)

> *He called you to this through our gospel that you might share in the glory of our Lord Jesus Christ.*
>
> 2 Thessalonians 2:14 (NIV)

God likes to share. He just does not like to be robbed. Though we could spend much time here, it is not the directive I have from His heart, so we will move forward.

My friend, the purpose of this coming into the light, this brief time of exposure, is never about the magnificence of the arrow, it is about revealing the purity of heart and intent of the arrow. When all is said and done, how do you respond when you begin to see your dream take flight? When destiny looms, will you remain faithful to the one who designed it, or will you forget His goodness?

I know we have shared this passage before, but I feel the need to share it again:

> *Make sure you don't forget God, your God, by not keeping his commandments, his rules and regulations that I command you today. Make sure that when you eat and are satisfied, build pleasant houses and settle in, see your herds and flocks flourish and more and more money come in, watch your standard of living going up and up - make sure*

72

you don't become so full of yourself and your things that you forget God, your God...

Deuteronomy 8:11

Remember God in all that you do. Take pleasure in the wind, spin fully in the elements, respond in joy to the flight, but make sure your rejoicing is in Him, your delight found solely in your union with The Archer. For this, dear arrow is a test that must be passed if you are ever to be used mightily, and perform precision strikes for the Kingdom.

Ah, can't you just feel the hope in that? Can't you sense the stirring in the heavens as you contemplate flying with the best and accomplishing all you can while on this planet?

Obedience, arrow. Obedience.

Humility, arrow. Humility.

It is all about Him. It is all to be done to His glory. Anything less is a diminished existence. I cannot imagine a better way of saying what Paul so eloquently stated:

And that's about it, friends. Be glad in God! I don't mind repeating what I have written in earlier letters, and I hope you don't mind hearing it again. Better safe than sorry – so here goes.

Steer clear of the barking dogs, those religious busybodies, all bark and no bite. All they're interested in is appearances – knife-happy circumcisers, I call them. The real believers are the ones the Spirit of God leads to work away at this ministry, filling the air with Christ's praise as we do it. We couldn't carry this off by our own efforts, and we know it – even though we can list what many might think are impressive credentials. You know my pedigree: a legitimate birth, circumcised on the eighth day; an Israelite from the

73

elite tribe of Benjamin; a strict and devout adherent to God's law; a fiery defender of the purity of my religion, even to the point of persecuting the church; a meticulous observer of everything set down in God's law Book.

The very credentials these people are waving around as something special, I'm tearing up and throwing out with the trash - along with everything else I used to take credit for.

And why? Because of Christ. Yes, all the things I once thought were so important are gone from my life. Compared to the high privilege of knowing Christ Jesus as my Master, firsthand, everything I once thought I had going for me is insignificant - dog dung. I've dumped it all in the trash so that I could embrace Christ and be embraced by him. I didn't want some petty, inferior brand of righteousness that comes from keeping a list of rules when I could get the robust kind that comes from trusting Christ - God's righteousness.

I gave up all that inferior stuff so I could know Christ personally, experience his resurrection power, be a partner in his suffering, and go all the way with him to death itself. If there was any way to get in on the resurrection from the dead, I wanted to do it.

I'm not saying that I have this all together, that I have it made. But I am well on my way, reaching out for Christ, who has so wondrously reached out for me. Friends, don't get me wrong: By no means do I count myself an expert in all of this, but I've got my eye on the goal, where God is beckoning us onward - to Jesus. I'm off and running, and I'm not turning back. So let's keep focused on that goal, those of us who want everything God has for us. If any of you have something else in mind, something less than total

74

Arrows in His Hand

commitment, God will clear your blurred vision – you'll see it yet! Now that we're on the right track, let's stay on it. Stick with me, friends. Keep track of those you see running this same course, headed for this same goal. There are many out there taking other paths, choosing other goals, and trying to get you to go along with them. I've warned you of them many times; sadly, I'm having to do it again. All they want is easy street. They hate Christ's Cross. But easy street is a dead-end street. Those who live there make their bellies their gods; belches are their praise; all they can think of is their appetites.

But there's far more to life for us. We're citizens of high heaven! We're waiting the arrival of the Savior, the Master, Jesus Christ, who will transform our earthy bodies into glorious bodies like his own. He'll make us beautiful and whole with the same powerful skill by which he is putting everything as it should be, under and around him.

Philippians 3:1-21

Everything truly is to be brought under and around Him. Your purpose and ultimate calling upon this planet is to bring Him glory, making His name huge in the earth. Small flight, minute exposition, and great journey alike, you glory in Him. Enjoy the privilege of flying by His hand, and quickly release all praise to the only One Who is due such things.

Ah, well trained arrow, savor this time of instruction. Get straight to the heart of it. For soon enough, dear one, your positioning will change, and in the blink of an eye you will find yourself facing the dirt from which you came.

Facedown

I sewed myself a shroud and wore it like a shirt;
I lay facedown in the dirt.
Now my face is blotched red from weeping;
*   look at the dark shadows under my eyes,*
Even though I've never hurt a soul
*   and my prayers are sincere!*

Job 16:15

What a trip! Positioned, chosen, tested for true, hidden, exposed - you now enter the next stage of the training process: Facedown. In practical archery positioning, this is where The Archer swings the arrow up and out of the quiver, only to bring it facedown as He places it securely upon the bow string.

I do not even know where to begin.

Please let me say this up front: Facedown does not imply that you have blown it. This is not a punishment; this is discipline. Two completely different things. We head into this chapter with the absolute wrong mindset if we think the arrow is being punished. The enemy would love to have you think that, for with punishment often comes shame. Man is prone to punish as retaliation. God is prone to discipline for purpose of training.

Punish: *a: to impose a penalty on for a fault, offense, or violation b: to inflict a penalty for the commission of (an offense) in retribution or retaliation*

2 a: to deal with roughly or harshly
b: to inflict injury on

Discipline: *to train or develop by instruction and exercise especially in self-control.*

See the vast difference? Let's take a few minutes and lay a scriptural foundation.

Blessed is the man whom God corrects; so do not despise the discipline of the Almighty.

Job 5:17 (NIV)

Blessed is the man you discipline, O LORD, the man you teach from your law; you grant him relief from days of trouble, till a pit is dug for the wicked.

Psalm 94:12,13 (NIV)

…because the LORD disciplines those he loves, as a father the son he delights in.

Proverbs 3:12 (NIV)

Facedown is a place of discipline. It is not a punishment. Just as discipline trains and brings self control, so does this stage of the positioning of the arrow. This is where the arrow gets locked into position and made ready to be brought up. It is *affixed* and clings to the bow string. Trained to stay in place until called up, we must see this as a time of wondrous stabilization.

Understand, you have probably done nothing wrong. You have most likely flown with grandeur, laying all glorious

77

crowns at His feet. You soared with the eagles for brief and beautiful moments, the wind lifting you above your circumstances, giving you a vantage point unlike any you had seen before. The sun shone, the watcher arrows applauded, the elements rushed by as you breathed deeply of His breath. Ah, it is at once marvelous, magnificent, grand and intoxicating, this view from the high places. But the high places can get you in trouble if you refuse to come down. We have a tendency to build altars to strange gods – or worship our own accomplishments - if we stay in the high places too long.

> *But they put God to the test and rebelled against the Most High; they did not keep his statutes. Like their fathers they were disloyal and faithless, as unreliable as a faulty bow. They angered him with their high places; they aroused his jealousy with their idols. When God heard them, he was very angry; he rejected Israel completely.*
>
> Psalm 78:56-59 (NIV)

> *Blessed are you, O Israel! Who is like you, a people saved by the LORD? He is your shield and helper and your glorious sword. Your enemies will cower before you, and you will trample down their high places.*
>
> Deuteronomy 33:29 (NIV)

But, I digress. Back to our key scripture.

> *The purity of silver and gold is tested by putting them in the fire; The purity of human hearts is tested by giving them a little fame.*
>
> Proverbs 27:21

There is something about the exposure flights of the arrow that bring out the Refiner in God. He becomes that overprotective parent that looks beyond the surface and peers beyond our "oh, everything went great" smiles. When our test flight ends, He takes the seat of the Refiner and begins to examine the arrow's heart to see how it came through the flight, and just what might have been exposed mid-air.

What is He looking for?

He looks to see if we hold onto the praise of the watcher arrows; if we have tucked it away and held on for a future pride-fest. Have we gloried in our accomplishment, or gloried in His having allowed our flight? Have we counted our flight an honor, or have we counted it a deserved earning; a wage or payback for all we have done for Him? Have we come in contact with anything that might have left us bent or off center? Have any impurities taken hold of our fletching?

> *The heart is hopelessly dark and deceitful, a puzzle that no one can figure out. But I, God, search the heart and examine the mind. I get to the heart of the human. I get to the root of things. I treat them as they really are, not as they pretend to be.*

> Jeremiah 17:9-10

When my husband examines the arrows he is going to use, I am often found shaking my head, thinking to myself, *There is not one thing wrong with that arrow he just set aside.* My untrained eye thinks it looks like all of the rest. But his trained eyes see what I cannot. He sees the smallest thing that could cause the arrow to deviate from course. A messed up fletching, a small dent in the shaft, a misshapen tip - each could cause the arrow to be ineffective in its journey. He does not blame the arrow for the imperfections; he simply sets them aside for correction and repair.

Arrows need small correction – refining - to fly with greatest effect. A spiritual arrow (you or I) is no different. There is maintenance that must take place in order for us to fly our best. God knows how to make these needed adjustments, but it may take a little heat to make the adjustment. He is faithful to sit as our Refiner and make sure the work is done.

Ah, Dear Archer and Refiner, do your work. Heat, shape and mold as you see fit. Make us useable. Make us straight arrows that fly and strike with precision.

From the heights to the depths, He is God. In flight or on foot, He is Lord. Let all be done to His greater glory. Let our soaring and our facedown moments (our humbling) be offered up to Him, for He is the lifter of our heads.

At this point in our instruction, having flown in fame or failure, the arrows are all brought to the same checkpoint. The Archer now reminds you of why you should be grateful to have flown, and gives you a divine revelation of just how lost you would be without Him.

In physical form, an archer will bring the arrow point-down, facing the ground, as he nocks it upon the bowstring. In the spirit, The Archer has just brought you to a place of humble gratitude. This can happen in so many ways. I have experienced this place in several ways but there are two that I find myself in most frequently:

Method 1 - Gentle Correction (because of a purposeful commitment to humility): Walking in deep gratitude every step of the way, allowing Him to instill a deep recognition of His grace over our lives, while fully acknowledging the dirt from which we have come.

Method 2: - Swift Discipline (based on a rebellious nature): Walking in pride and basking in the attention gained on flights, while taking liberties with the glory that belongs to God, and experiencing in turn the speedy and effective discipline of the facedown instruction.

If we are wise, we will realize that every single one of us are quite capable of being brought low for both reasons - and the choice is usually ours. God brings us facedown not for the purpose of shaming, but of taming. He brings us down from our high places so that we will remember His goodness and respect His commands. He brings low in order to birth reverence and re-establish His God-ness in our hearts. He allows us to glory in His greatness as we catch brief glimpses of how desolate our lives would have been without His rich mercies and timely intervention.

Ah, Arrow, humility must come in this stage of the revelation. If it does not, you may just experience the hiding place (quiver) again. The experience of exposure and flight may puff you up - *Look what I did! I went high and moved through the elements with lightning speed.* Let's be sure to remind ourselves regularly that all arrow movement is inspired by the hand of The Archer.

When my boys were little, it seemed I was always buying tennis shoes. They wore them out as soon as I bought them (I know the moms and dads are nodding their heads). My beautiful sons of thunder (James Aaron and Jon Matthew) had much to do and even more to see; so many grand adventures to experience, they were forever wearing out their shoes or outgrowing them. I find it all so very precious in hindsight. What a privilege we have, this putting of shoes on little feet.

Let's move forward before this mother's heart gets quite melancholy.

Ah yes, the buying of shoes. The same scene played out every single time I bought new shoes. The boys always believed they could run faster and jump higher because of the shoes. They would leap and run down the aisles of the store as I did the "Oh, my goodness! That was way too fast and high!" mom thing. They were so amazed at the magic of the shoes that allowed them to do those magnificent record breaking feats. Those were some amazing shoes!

Oh, but let me tell you, those magnificent shoes would not have jumped, ran or leapt even once without the precious little feet that filled them. How foolish it would have been for the shoes to take the glory for the feet that danced within them. And how foolish it would be for the arrow to claim the glory of The Archer who brings them to life.

I believe the lesson of this facedown stage is very simply a deep and divine revelation of God's sovereignty and a profound understanding of His extravagant grace over the life of the arrow.

Friend, when The Archer begins to bring you out of the hidden places, never forget the hand that made it happen. I know you are probably thinking you could never forget how good God has been to you. Still, God does not address and speak to that which need not be addressed. He does not waste words and talk about random things and nonsense that may or may not take place. If He took the time to share with us safeguards and instructions regarding humility and honor, it is because He knew we would have need of them. I find such safeguards reassuring and foundational as it relates to our remembering how we arrived in our good land or stuck the mark.

You see, God knew the heart of man would have a tendency toward forgetting Him when things were going well. Yes, we would remember and call out in our distress, but in the blessings and times of ease, we easily go about our own business and forget the business was His in the first place. God does not want that to happen. The Archer wants the arrow to remember and be thankful. He knows it is the best thing for us.

I would like you to take just a moment and read the continuation of the passage you found earlier in this chapter. Read it until it speaks to your heart. Do not move on quickly, but allow God to plant it within a heart that has tendencies toward self-focus.

> *So it's paramount that you keep the commandments of God, your God, walk down the roads he shows you and reverently respect him. God is about to bring you into a good land, a land with brooks and rivers, springs and lakes, streams out of the hills and through the valleys. It's a land of wheat and barley, of vines and figs and pomegranates, of olives, oil, and honey. It's land where you'll never go hungry – always food on the table and a roof over your head. It's a land where you'll get iron out of rocks and mine copper from the hills.*
>
> *After a meal, satisfied, bless God, your God, for the good land he has given you.*
>
> *Make sure you don't forget God, your God, by not keeping his commandments, his rules and regulations that I*

command you today. Make sure that when you eat and are satisfied, build pleasant houses and settle in, see your herds and flocks flourish and more and more money come in, watch your standard of living going up and up – make sure you don't become so full of yourself and your things that you forget God, your God, the God who delivered you from Egyptian slavery; the God who led you through that huge and fearsome wilderness, those desolate, arid badlands crawling with fiery snakes and scorpions; the God who gave you water gushing from hard rock; the God who gave you manna to eat in the wilderness, something your ancestors had never heard of, in order to give you a taste of the hard life, to test you so that you would be prepared to live well in the days ahead of you.

If you start thinking to yourselves, "I did all this. And all by myself. I'm rich. It's all mine!" – well, think again. Remember that God, your God, gave you the strength to produce all this wealth so as to confirm the covenant that he promised to your ancestors – as it is today.

If you forget, forget God, your God, and start taking up with other gods, serving and worshiping them, I'm on record right now as giving you firm warning: that will be the end of you; I mean it – destruction. You'll go to your doom – the same as the nations God is destroying before you; doom because you wouldn't obey the Voice of God, your God.

Deuteronomy 8:6-20

As I prayed about this, the conviction of my heart was that most are willing to fly, but few return the glory to where it belongs; few return just to say thank you. Once we fly, we forget how we flew. We stroke our own feathers and admire the scenery, forgetting the Strong Arm that pulled back that bowstring. I sensed the Father speaking to my spirit, saying, "They all want to fly, but few faithfully return to the bow." Though unspoken, I knew the Spirit of the Lord was saying… "and unless they do, the one small insignificant flight is all they will ever experience at My hand. If they do not return in humility, the lifting and promotion of the next step will never happen."

Facedown infers humility. Facedown, by physical position alone, denotes submission and surrender. Facedown, He establishes Who He is, and who we are. His heart mingles with ours and we are known, through and through. As a subject bows before the King, so the arrow must bow before The Archer; in recognition of the absolute honor due Him. In this, the arrow declares The Archer Lord, and vows fealty to Him, saying with Isaiah, "Here I am Lord, send me."

You know, I have always had a bit of a problem with all of the "who I am in Christ" teachings. There was just something about that which rubbed the wrong way. You know, kind of like petting a cat in the wrong direction. It sounded good on the surface, and for a while I could not put my finger on what bothered me about this particular teaching. Then one day while reading the scriptures, I finally figured it out. I understood what it was that felt like a splinter under my skin.

> *To them God has chosen to make known among the Gentiles the glorious riches of this mystery, which is Christ in you, the hope of glory.*

> Colossians 1:27 (NIV)

Our lives are not about who we are in Him, but Who He is in us. That changes everything. Our focus is no longer fixed on who we are, but Who He is. Now, that is a worthy thought; a worthy pursuit of knowledge. That is something worth rejoicing in. Focusing on who we are is distracting, and can birth self-inflation. Maintaining correct focus on Him, well, it keeps you humble. He is quite awesome, you know. Anything that keeps your eyes on Him, keeps you somehow in proper perspective. Stick with me here. It is this facedown dirt time which helps us keep a proper perspective. Christ in us, the hope of glory. We must not focus on the arrow, but The Archer.

Ah, facedown consultation before Archer feet. Love it! Whole new vantage point.

I have what many might call a very active imagination, but I choose to call *keen visionary instincts* (I like that!). Just the thought of swinging low and coming near the feet of The Archer sets my spirit to trembling. I cannot help but think about what I might actually see when coming that close to His precious feet, what I might sense in such close proximity. Perhaps in those moments I might glimpse the path He has walked, and know the foolishness found upon my own. What if, for fleeting moments, the scars of the battle He wages find their way into my line of vision?

Oh, can you let your spirit journey with me for a moment and, in doing so, gain a broader vision of this particular positioning in the instruction of the arrow? Facedown is preparation time. Facedown, you are undistracted and intimately connected to the hand of The Archer. Facedown, you see that from which The Archer created you, and to what your flesh one day will return.

The tendency, when we have flown well, is to think that no correction, adjustment or discipline is needed. But God knows us so well. He knows what can happen to the human heart when it receives glory. He is not going to let that happen to His arrows.

I know, we have flown well, and given glory to The Archer for all that we have accomplished through His hand, but still, the Master Archer searches the heart of the little arrow. This is pure maintenance and simple discipline.

The Archer is all about keeping an eye on the wholeness of the arrow. Just as we (if wise) have yearly physicals to maintain our health, we must have spiritual wellness exams, as well; checkpoints, for lack of better wording.

The Archer knows that one of the greatest temptations of the arrow is to give in to the elements and choose its own course. If not held by a firm grip (kept humble), and directed by The Master Archer (listening closely), an arrow can easily fly off target. It doesn't take a huge deviation (just one good look at how pretty it looks in flight or a little too much attention given to the applause of the watchers) for an arrow to find itself way off center. Still, even those arrows that get it right, giving all glory and honor to Him during their brief time in the spotlight, will find themselves facedown. It is the stabilizing point of the instruction of the arrow. You will never bypass this step in any flight. Period. Reject it, and you will go nowhere. Trust me in this.

Check yourself often in the areas of humility and grace. Make sure you keep your flesh under control and your pride in submission. Again, the haughty arrow will quickly taste dust. Correction comes swiftly in the form of sudden impact with terra firma. In other words, your flight ends abruptly. That beautiful thing you took credit for, the ministry, the class, the relationships, the victories, swiftly falls apart when it is left solely up to you to complete it or keep it going. When the anointing of God, The Archer, is removed from what you have set your hands to, you just may be amazed at how instantaneously it all turns to dust.

Remember: if you send you, you must maintain your own position. If He sends you, He alone will keep you in place. Which would you prefer? I mean, really, my friend, an arrow looks pretty ridiculous trying to throw itself - and it doesn't get very far. The great similarity between the faithful and unfaithful arrow is that they both are affected by the dirt. The good arrow is brought facedown and views it, by the natural movement of The Archer's arm. The bad tastes its folly; the good sees the dirt, but does not make contact with it. The sight alone is enough to bring a call to discipline, and a birthing of renewed gratitude.

Does that make sense to you? The bad arrow goes face first into the dirt because of its rebellion, while the good arrow comes over the shoulder of The Archer, and swings down to face the dirt from which it came and is kept humble in the process. Similar in position, but entirely different in purpose.

In the following scriptures you just may find out why you are in this particular phase.

And you, Solomon my son, get to know well your father's God; serve him with a whole heart and eager mind, for God examines every heart and sees through every motive. If you seek him, he'll make sure you find him, but if you abandon him, he'll leave you for good. Look sharp now! God has chosen you to build his holy house. Be brave, determined! And do it!

I Chronicles 28:9-10

> *Meanwhile, the moment we get tired in the waiting, God's Spirit is right alongside helping us along. If we don't know how or what to pray, it doesn't matter. He does our praying in and for us, making prayer out of our wordless sighs, our aching groans. He knows us far better than we know ourselves, knows our pregnant condition, and keeps us present before God. That's why we can be so sure that every detail in our lives of love for God is worked into something good.*

Romans 8:26-28

But, I do not need my heart checked! I do not need to be searched! Yes, dear one, we all need to have our hearts searched on a regular basis, for as The Archer so eloquently reminds us:

> *The heart is hopelessly dark and deceitful, a puzzle that no one can figure out. But I, God, search the heart and examine the mind. I get to the heart of the human. I get to the root of things. I treat them as they really are, not as they pretend to be.*

Jeremiah 17:9-10

The facedown positioning is a life-changer, but it is not the woe-is-me position many assume it is when first broached. This is a position of expectation and coming ascent. It is actually full of hope and bathed in reverence. Still, many will glimpse the chapter title and assume a sackcloth and ashes demeanor.

Inevitably, when I teach this series in churches, I wind up with at least half of the congregation thinking they are in this particular phase in the instruction of the arrow. I get tickled sometimes. Somber faced congregants come up to shake my hand or ask for prayer, and they tell me, "Oh, sister, I am facedown. I spent most of my life facedown; it's a struggle, you know." I used to fight the urge to say, "Then let Him do what needs to be done so you can get on with it. There is work to be done!"

I no longer fight that urge. Guess that could explain why I am not invited back for round two? Perhaps that is why I am in my home church instead of on the road at this moment (Selah). Not many can take a "Get out of the dirt" message. Ah, but you must be able to take it, for He has placed this in your hands.

I reiterate, facedown is for discipline, instruction and re-establishment of humility. Facedown is not the punishment phase so many assume it is. This is when the arrow learns where to lay the crowns of victory that will unerringly come to those willing to receive instruction and become disciplined in the hand of The Archer.

You might be in this phase of instruction if:

> You feel like you just fell from grace.
> You know the pull of opening up every area of your life to the gaze of The Archer.
> You are having a great battle with pride issues.
> You see no forward motion in your walk with Christ, but you long to get everything in order so that movement might come.
> You vacillate between conviction and condemnation. God is teaching you the difference between the two.
> You know He had you in a strong grip, but you are not sure why.
> You are reminded of your past, but only as a backdrop for how far you have come.

You are very sensitive to dirt (small sin issues you once were able to get by with / ignore).
Your prayer life has become full of tears.
You cannot worship without falling to your knees.
You cannot get enough of Him.

Ask God (The Archer) to reveal your heart, and show you clearly if this is where you are. Ask Him to show you what you need to do to move forward. Open your heart to instruction. Travail with tears. Worship from a heart full of recognition of His greatness. Let His hand position you on the bowstring.

A marvelous thing is taking place. You are going to feel grounded and established. You will find yourself becoming genuinely stable in your faith; knowing an unshakable firmness in your walk. When this happens, know that you are on the precipice of being nocked upon the bow, and in this, you can know that promotion is most assuredly coming.

In the words of T.D. Jakes, "Get ready! Get ready! Get ready!"

Promoted and Aligned

When God, who is the best shepherd of all, comes out in the open with his rule, he'll see that you've done it right and commend you lavishly. And you who are younger must follow your leaders. But all of you, leaders and followers alike, are to be down to earth with each other, for – God has had it with the proud, But takes delight in just plain people. So be content with who you are, and don't put on airs. God's strong hand is on you; he'll promote you at the right time.

1 Peter 5:4-7

We give praise and thanks to You, O God, we praise and give thanks; Your wondrous works declare that Your Name is near and they who invoke Your Name rehearse Your wonders. When the proper time has come [for executing My judgments], I will judge uprightly [says the Lord]. When the earth totters, and all the inhabitants of it, it is I Who will poise and keep steady its pillars. Selah [pause, and calmly think of that]! I said to the arrogant and boastful, Deal not arrogantly [do not boast]; and to the wicked, Lift not up the horn [of personal aggrandizement]. Lift not up your [aggressive] horn on high, speak not with a stiff neck and insolent arrogance. For not from the east nor from the west nor from the south come promotion and lifting up.

> *But God is the Judge! He puts down one and lifts up another.*
>
> Psalm 75:1-7 (AMP)

All promotion comes from God. No one else can raise you up and position you in stability. God alone does good things such as this. He is great like that. The stage into which we now enter demands a settling of this issue. He alone has birthed this promotion in your life. If you are being lifted through the ranks, it is because He has chosen to do so. Never forget what He has done. Or, as my granny was fond of saying - "Girl, you'd best dance with the one what brung ya!" That was her way of reminding me of how good God has been to me; reminding me of where I would be if not for Him - telling me to hold on tight in the midst of the spin... and dance with the God Who made my feet able to move. It was also her way of letting me know that she knew what I was like before Jesus. One shake of that little finger was all I needed to step back into the dance. She could remind me of my error while assuring me of her great love. Sounds like someone else I know.

I loved my grandmother. She was a mess. What a wonderful gift God has given us, friends and family who remind us that we owe everything we are to God. May we never be without companions such as these!

Now, let's talk about some arrows.

Having learned the lessons of being chosen, tested, hidden, exposed and facedown, you now enter into a new and wonderful phase of the instruction of the arrow: promotion and alignment.

Yes!

Everyone likes a little promotion from time to time. Alignment? Well, that may be a different story, but we are ready for that, as well. So, let's journey (or dance)!

Promoted: *to advance in station, rank, or honor.*

Oh, of all of these, may my promotion be in areas of honor - not that I would be honored, but that I would be honorable and grow in my understanding of truly honoring this God Whom we serve. Reverence, honor, respect: let us be forever promoted in these areas.

Time to breathe. Time to lift your head. Time to set your eyes on the horizon. God is bringing you up. Steady... steady... no time for fear... just divine hope and great attentiveness.

When The Archer searches the heart of the arrow and finds humility, love, obedience and submission, He does something profoundly stabilizing for the arrow; He brings it (as leaving the facedown position) onto the nocking point. He locks the arrow onto the bow. Think about it; if you do the work of the facedown teaching, you come out more stable than you have ever been. Who doesn't want that?

The problem is that very few are willing to walk through *facedown* to get to *stable*. Can I say that again? Too few are willing to walk through the humbling facedown position in order to get to the promotional instruction.

They are waiting for another magic formula; something that does not require tears or travail. But facedown is facedown. You may arise with a bit of dirt in your eyebrows, but do not worry - a little dirt looks good on stable eyebrows.

Stability; how we have longed for this! We have been tested, handled, crowded, jostled, humbled and finally (yes, finally), stabilized. Wishy-washy arrow has left the building! Boy, it is about time.

This is so cool! Up to this point, Archer, bow and arrow have not been fully joined in purpose for any length of time, but in the facedown position, the three unite. *Can I get an Ah, Jesus!?*

The Archer, His bow (method of delivery), and the arrow, find agreement, and become joined in a new way. New strength and direction come into the arrow. Now, when the bow (method of delivery) lifts its head, the arrow automatically rises with it.

In the temporal flesh realm, the bow (method of delivery and positioning) may look like a new position, or a new opportunity. In fact, though you probably do not want to hear this, the bow very often looks entirely like opposition, suffering or hardship.

Wait! Don't shut the book yet.

Promotion, opportunity and opposition have always been linked. It's why many people do not like their bosses or leaders... undermining or maligning them. Satan sends opposition where there is promotion or opportunity. Let's hope that you have never been a part of his schemes to undermine authority and those promoted by God!

Okay, I did not intend for us to go there, but now that we have I think we need to address this issue with our Father. If you have been guilty of tearing down leadership at home, at work, at church, you need to repent and ask God to forgive you. You have been in opposition to the door of opportunity

God opened in their lives. You need to turn away from that attitude, blessing and not cursing those who have been placed over you in any of these areas.

You see, Satan so opposes open doors of service, that God, in His great wisdom made opposition a doorway in and of itself. Opposition became a gateway to spiritual promotion. Think about it. Every time you face opposition you have an opportunity to grow and become greater in the kingdom.

I love when He does stuff like that! Now we can look at opposition and say, "Hey, Look! Another open door of opportunity!"

I must tell you, this one gets me. When I think about how many times I have rebuked Satan for a work God was trying to complete in me, I find it very disheartening. How much could God have accomplished in this life if I had not run from and avoided any kind of opposition? I thought I was avoiding strife, when in truth, I was avoiding my issues. God had been trying to get me to stand up for years before I actually had the peace to do so.

Does that hit home with anyone besides me? How many times, when faced with opposition, have we backed down or compromised because of the pressure? How many times have we allowed opposition to close our doors? Promotion did not come easy, so we gave up. How many times have we let obstacles stop us, failing to see the opportunity in clearing the hurdle? The Word tells us that with opportunity, there is opposition.

> *A huge door of opportunity for good work has opened up here. (There is also mushrooming opposition.)*
> 1 Corinthians 16:9

We need a new mindset. We need to understand that opposition merely lets us know that opportunity is before us. We need to begin to see it as a road sign saying:

Door of Opportunity Ahead!

Ah, how liberating would that be? Yes, a new mindset is needed for this, and only one thing can actually change our minds and renew our mindsets: say it with me - The Word of God.

In this promotional phase of instruction the arrow becomes stable, faithful and humble, regardless of surroundings or opposition. We know what the Word says about being humble in His hand.

> *Humble yourselves, therefore, under God's mighty hand, that he may lift you up in due time.*

> I Peter 5:6 (NIV)

Darlin' it is due time!

The Archer is getting ready to bring the arrow up. You may not feel like you are coming up. If truth were known, you may actually feel, locked into the delivery system as you are, as if your wings have been clipped, your freedom diminished. Ah, but things are not as they appear, or even as they may feel. In the spirit, you have just found the stability of the bow. You have been affixed, centered, stabilized and now rest fully on, you guessed it... the rest of the bow.

You are in the midst of profound change, and even struggle, but as is the way of our Archer, He has stabilized you and even given you a place of rest in the raising. To me, the beauty of this is that in attaching us, and giving us a place of rest, all weight is actually taken off of the arrow, and all lifting and promotion is absolutely accomplished and completed by The Archer. The arrow has no control at this point. The Archer now has full and complete control.

Took a while to get here, didn't it? I don't know about you, but the thought of all weight and pressure being removed for the moment sounds wonderful to me. You know things are going on, but it is beyond your control; so you actually find a place of rest.

Have you ever been there? Everything around you is shifting and changing and you come to the realization that you cannot do a thing about any of it? It is as if things just took on a life of their own and you are just a spectator to all that is happening in you life. Still, you have peace. Nothing is like it once was, but you are not shaken. You are still resting in Him, and you feel somehow, unexplainably stable in your walk.

You are being promoted. It has not happened as you expected. There are no accolades, corner offices or pay increases, but you have just been given a new position: stable and peaceful. Do you understand how very blessed you are? Do you understand how many people spend their entire lives trying to achieve this position? This is no small thing. You are being moved and promoted by the hand of The Archer alone. Amazing!

Something transcendent sparks through the arrow; upward momentum. Yes! (This accompanied by the pumping of the bent right arm in an up and down motion.) Bliss! No more dirt (at least for the time being). From bowed to buoyant. *It's too much! I jus can't take no mo...* (A little James Brown can be cathartic.)

There is nothing like being moved up and promoted by God. If God promotes you and places you in the position He wants you in; then only God can take you out of it. It takes all of the performance pressure off of you. If He has brought you here, He has made you ready to stand in this place. You might feel like you are in over your head, but you are never in over His.

> *Don't work yourself into the spotlight; don't push your way into the place of prominence. It's better to be promoted to a place of honor than face humiliation by being demoted.*
>
> Proverbs 25:6-7

When the arrow begins to be lifted from the facedown position, it is not brought up on its own initiative. The arrow comes up only by His hand. Are you beginning to get the true picture; everything is by His hand. He chooses, He tests, He hides away, He exposes, He brings humility, and He is the only source of true promotion. His hand; how blessed to be found there.

> *God brings death and God brings life, brings down to the grave and raises up. God brings poverty and God brings wealth; he lowers, he also lifts up. He puts poor people on their feet again; he rekindles burned-out lives with fresh hope, Restoring dignity and respect to their lives – a place in the sun! For the very structures of earth are God's; he has laid out his operations on a firm foundation. He protectively cares for his faithful friends, step by step, but leaves the wicked to stumble in the dark. No one makes it in this life by sheer muscle! God's enemies will be blasted out of the sky, crashed in a heap and burned. God will set things right all over the earth, he'll give strength to his king, he'll set his anointed on top of the world!*
>
> 1 Samuel 2:6-10

When was the last time you felt the small and miniscule adjustments of the Holy Spirit in your life? Did you submit to them? My sharp friend, exult! Take great pleasure in His instruction as He raises you. This is such a wondrous time for you. This is the time, when in the physical you might be teaching a class, instructing students, training your spirit and disciplining your flesh.

Again, probably not what you wanted to hear. But let me give you a word of encouragement here; if God has opened a door for you to serve, serve faithfully. If you are teaching, study more than you think you need to. If you are serving in helps, truly be of help. Do not choose where you will serve, just make the offer and leave the assignments and results wide open. Do more than required. Take initiative and exceed expectation. For, my friend, we have moved from the place of functioning at acceptable, and stepped into a level of accountability which asks us to function in excellence.

After all, God has called and equipped, and He does nothing with mediocrity. During this promotion you are brought up in levels of understanding, depths of wisdom, interpretation of Scripture. I believe this is the time in the instruction of the arrow that the Ephesians 1 prayer begins to manifest in richness.

I keep asking that the God of our Lord Jesus Christ, the glorious Father, may give you the Spirit of wisdom and revelation, so that you may know him better. I pray also that the eyes of your heart may be enlightened in order that you may know the hope to which he has called you, the riches of his glorious inheritance in the saints.

Ephesians 1:17-18 (NIV)

God has taken you through humility into revelation. Who knew promotion came through the humble places? I mean, in this world, promotion comes through fighting and clawing your way to the top, right? How like our God to make promotion a matter of the heart, flowing from a place of humility, service and profound gratitude. I just love Him! He goes against the systems of the world and brings a greater result. He is such a wonderful God.

God-promotion: this is the time when your faith in The Archer is renewed and strengthened. You are advancing, though there is no fast-forward movement as of yet. You are now being asked to trust and obey on so many levels, for, as is His way, in being promoted kingdom-wise, you are most likely responsible for more than yourself. You feel a new sense of responsibility; know a greater need to get it right. For now your journey has been intricately intermingled with the flights of the other arrows, and you know that everything you do has an effect on the others. Still, peace and stability have infused you.

Many marks have now come into your sphere of influence. He has equipped you to strike wherever He sends you, opened so many doors of opportunity. At this time you cannot see your exact target (your destined mark), and due to His motion / His working behind the scenes, your line of vision keeps changing. You feel a restlessness begin to course through you, and you have to settle yourself again. There is a part of you that fears this might be just another small test flight, that this cannot possibly be what you have been longing for; but the heart of you, the deepest places within you, know this time is divinely different. You know in the depths of who you are that everything you ever thought you knew is getting ready to change. You are being brought up,

101

promoted and aligned for a very specific purpose. You feel the hand of The Archer adjusting His grip.

Horizon changes. Focus becomes clearer. Thinks look different from this locked in vantage point. You do not feel unstable, or unsure. In fact, you have found a place of trust that you have never experienced before. You know that The Archer has you. You have known His touch before, but this is very different.

Let me explain. In this process you have experienced His touch on very different levels (man, this could birth another book!):

The touch of the Kinsman Redeemer: When chosen, you felt special, set-apart. His touch was gentle, selective.

The touch of the Great Physician: Selected, you knew the intimate touch that examines, searches, gives diagnosis and brings healing.

The touch of the Almighty (under the shadow of): He hid you away in safety, nurturing you in fortified places, teaching you to love and serve.

The touch of the Deliverer: Released from the confines of the quiver, He brought you out and let you soar.

The touch of the Faithful Father: Tender correction, wise discipline.

But this touch; you have not known this touch before. This touch of His hand sends strength and God-confidence surging through you.

The hand that now brings you up for battle is the hand of The Mighty Warrior. The hand that stabilizes you at this very moment is one that has fought many battles, coming through victorious in each. (Oh, I just want to find a piece of carpet right now and throw down!)

Does that not do something to you, to know that the hand that holds you right now held David as he ran toward Goliath; and held Joshua as he made that last lap around Jericho? The hand that holds you sends chariots of fire to claim triumphant prophets, and rolls seas back to stand upon themselves. This, my well-equipped arrow, is the ageless, timeless, undefeated touch of The Master.

Valor, honor, integrity, faithfulness, righteousness are His alone, and now rush like a wild thing through you. Oh, help us Father to understand what is going on at this very moment. The hand of The Archer / Warrior surrounds us, and with His strength, wisdom, passion, and experience, He begins to do something needed and necessary: His greatness aligns us.

Aligned: to be in or come into precise adjustment or correct relative position.

Precise adjustment, isn't that just what you wanted? Spiritual chiropractics. You are a little off here... Snap! Wait, relax... don't let this scare you... Crackle! Let's see, just a slight adjustment here... Pop! And with the flexing of His powerful hand, you just became an aligned arrow... or a breakfast cereal. (Get it? Snap, crackle, pop...) Sorry, couldn't resist!

You want to hear something really interesting? One of the most advanced archery tools now on the market is an alignment device. It helps the archer make sure the arrow is properly aligned by checking it against a concentrated beam of light. Hmmmm. Aligning an arrow by allowing it's trajectory to be determined by a light source alone. Sounds like a pretty good idea to me. What do you think?

Been there, done that!

Ah, friend, so many think promotion is easy, and that once lifted you have somehow arrived, when, in fact, once promoted, your journey only becomes more intricate and involved. Obedience is more important now than ever before. Accountability is now your companion and you answer for far more than your actions. Your motives now lay bare. If the truth were known, you may actually find yourself longing for the hidden places of yesterday's quiver.

Am I trying to discourage you? No. I want you to be fully equipped. As mature adults we have all invested ourselves in goals, positions or purposes that weren't quite all we expected when finally achieved or attained. I do not want you to be unaware. Promotion has its rewards and its pitfalls. You need to be ready for both.

So, here you go. Up you swing, the strong arm of The Archer directing your ascent. Full and expectant, you rise as He provides the impetus and opens the doors. Whew! You can finally begin to focus, catching brief glimpses of the mark toward which you will be sent. While now aligned and aimed in the general vicinity of your destined mark, you do not see it fully. The strike point is most definitely before you, but alignment has not been fully completed, so clarity escapes you. Still, you sense the concentration of The Archer, and you know He will complete what He has begun. You are fully assured that at any moment your long awaited bull's-eye will materialize before you. Stable, secure, peaceful, but taught with suspense, you submit; knowing that the slightest adjustment is made in mercy and for the preparation of the arrow.

Many would love to wiggle here. You think you know where you are going and think you know what needs to be done. You think you get it, are pretty sure you have this thing in the bag... and you want God to hurry and finish this alignment. Though you would love to position yourself, aligning yourself with what you see, if you do that, you are going to miss this much needed process, and very likely miss the target. A wise arrow will respect the vantage point of The Archer and surrender to an even greater extent. You thought you had nothing left in you to offer up, but there it is... sneaky little snake rears its head in the form of a desire to self-position. You do not even think twice; you release it.

No more self-will. No more self-adjustment. It's all Him now. Everything about you and your flight are completely and totally dependent upon Him... and all is as it should be.

Now a wonderful thing happens: fully submitted, you come fully awake and fully alert. You are quickened and ready to fly; you wait with great expectation; never losing hope, or vision.

> *Oh! May the God of green hope fill you up with joy, fill you up with peace, so that your believing lives, filled with the life-giving energy of the Holy Spirit, will brim over with hope!*

Romans 15:13 (MSG)

Friend, take every opportunity given to align yourself under the hand of this Mighty Warrior. Everything He tells you to do, do it. Just make the decision now to respond with "Yes, Sir!" Do not debate the issues, submit. Do not argue with

God, just rest in His wisdom. Trust that He will get you through this thing in perfect order. You do not have to understand all that is taking place. You do not need all of the answers. You simply require a heart that is willing to go wherever God says go, and be aligned as He sees fit.

I know in my spirit that so very many of you are here. You have submitted to the process, known His hand, His testing, His hiding place, His exposure, and His humbling, and because of your submission, revelation has come, and you are now experiencing a time of great promotion. He is bringing you into alignment with His will for you. He is lifting you.

He has brought down rulers from their thrones but has lifted up the humble.

Luke 1:52 (NIV)

The key to continued promotion and alignment is continued humility, and constant trust. You are coming up... He is getting ready to send you out. My precious friend, you truly want the lessons of this stage. You should earnestly desire the smallest tweaking and correction, for it is all to your benefit. He has your best interests at heart. How wonderful to be able to say that about someone and know it is absolute truth. He is concerned about you. He is making sure all is in readiness for your flight. Your buzz words (words that trigger a spirit response) need to be: adjustable, trainable, tender, submitted, peaceful, and aligned.

You may be in this level of arrow instruction if:

You are humbly aware of your past, yet intensely focused on your future.
You feel taught with expectancy, yet random in focus.
Unexpected kingdom opportunities have arisen.

106

You are finally willing to serve in unseen areas.

Your spiritual progress is being noted by those who are in positions to help you advance, but that is no longer important to you.

The eternity written upon your heart seems to be calling you out quite specifically.

You have a deep need to be about The Father's business.

You are keenly sensitized to the slightest movement of The Archer's hand.

Spiritual discernment has increased.

You feel stable for the first time in a long time.

You are finally getting a sense of what you are destined to accomplish in the earth.

You are at once tightly strung and perfectly at rest.

Hold on tightly, my friend. You are so very close to winging through the heavens, but you must first receive final instructions for flight. Promoted and aligned, everything is at the ready. You are chomping at the proverbial bit, ready to soar. You have now entered the stage of final preparation. You feel The Archer's grip tighten as you are...

Drawn Back

Drawn Back

He fills his hands with lightning and commands it to strike its mark.

Job 36:32 (NIV)

Have you ever been going along wonderfully, gaining ground, pushing in the spirit, taking new territory, walking in fullness, only to have everything stop in its tracks? All is great. The Spirit is moving. You know God is promoting you and moving you higher (or deeper) into the things of the Spirit, when suddenly you feel as if your head hits the proverbial spiritual boundary ceiling. Everything gets still. All is silent.

Been there? Of course you have. I truly believe we have all been there. We think it is some kind of limit God has placed on our spiritual progress. We have been here so many times it is ridiculous.

This is the place where many become extremely frustrated. This is the "nothing ever changes, this is exactly what happened last time" moment. This is the place where the enemy's voice reminds you of how many times you have banged your head against this ceiling. This is where he attempts to convince you that there is nothing beyond this particular barrier.

Aggravated, but feeling somehow holy and a tad superior, we must find someone or something to blame for this ceiling. Our first choice? The local church.

Of course! It must be our church and its leadership. We decide that our progress has been impeded, the ceiling put in place by our pastor. When we are pulled back spiritually, it must be our pastor's fault. But then again, it could be our friends or our mates. We examine their shortcomings. *"Well, he just doesn't let the spirit flow like he should. This church does not operate in the gifts (this assuming others and not you should operate in the gifts). They quench the breakthrough spirit."*

Please! When did *They* (whoever *they* are) become responsible for your personal relationship with Christ? When did *they* muzzle you and tie your hands, keeping you from laying hands on the sick, or prophesying under God's anointing? When did *they* become so empowered that *they* can stop God's move in your life?

You know, I am a tolerant person, but one thing I will not tolerate is this whole spiritual blame-game. The Word tells us to "work out our own salvation with fear and trembling."

> *Therefore, my dear friends, as you have always obeyed - not only in my presence, but now much more in my absence - continue to work out your salvation with fear and trembling, for it is God who works in you to will and to act according to his good purpose.*
>
> Philippians 2:12-13 (NIV)

You are where you are in your walk with Christ because you have chosen to be there. Friend, your obedience has nothing to do with the obedience of others, nor does your level of faith. Faith and obedience are completely personal. God will not ask you what I did with my life, but what you did with yours. Excuses carry no weight in eternal balances.

When you hit this perceived ceiling, understand, you are going to hear two voices: one telling you there is no passing beyond this point, another saying:

> *This is God's Message, the God who made earth, made it livable and lasting, known everywhere as God: 'Call to me and I will answer you. I'll tell you marvelous and wondrous things that you could never figure out on your own.'*
>
> Jeremiah 33:2-3

Which voice will you listen to? Experience may tell you that the ceiling is your limit, but God says there is no limit. Are you going to do what the scripture says and call to Him, or will you lean once again on your own understanding?

> *Trust God from the bottom of your heart; don't try to figure out everything on your own. Listen for God's voice in everything you do, everywhere you go; he's the one who will keep you on track. Don't assume that you know it all.*
>
> Proverbs 3:5-6

You are at the "don't assume you know it all" stage of the journey. You can stop here again, or you can begin to call out to Him in a deeper more specific way, acknowledging Him in every single breath. I do not know about your Bible, but mine tells me that if I will do those things, He will answer me, telling me marvelous and wondrous things that I have never been able to figure out before... like how to move beyond this place.

Wouldn't you love some answers? I mean, really, wherever you are, whatever phase of instruction you might find yourself in, wouldn't you like to know how to move forward? As much as I would love to give a profound and insightful answer, I can give it to you in two words - words that have absolutely revolutionized my walk with Christ; common, ordinary words that absolutely carry the seed and DNA of enormous spiritual breakthrough: *Submit* and *Attend*.

> **Submit:** *to yield oneself to the authority or will of another: to defer to or consent to abide by the opinion or authority of another.*

> **Attend:** *to pay attention to, to look after, to go or stay with as a companion, nurse, or servant: to wait for, to be in store for, to be present with, accompany: to be present, to apply oneself, to apply the mind or pay attention: to be ready for service, wait, stay: to direct one's attention toward.*

Submit and attend: bow your will. Surrender control. Become fully available to wait upon Him. In the midst of ceiling hitting seasons, it is time to listen, to be still and know that He is God, to wait and attend.

In the journey of the arrow, you have just come through the promotion phase. The Archer has raised you up from your former realities and given you a whole new perspective. The raising, however, has come to a stop, and the drawing back has now begun. It is time to submit to the drawing, to be fully present and to listen. Frustration at the head bump cannot be in this moment with you. Stop and listen.

Get ready, my friend, your God, the Master Archer, has drawn you back for final instruction.

Can I get an, *Ah, Jesus!*

Called, chosen, tested, hidden, exposed, facedown, promoted and aligned, you now move into the final phase of your preparation for this particular journey. I cannot tell you how much this phase rocks me.

There is enough of a dreamer inside of me that I cannot help but think about what The Archer is doing at this particular moment. He has walked you through this entire process with a specific result in mind – the striking of the mark. As He draws you back for final instruction, can you just imagine that His eyes are set on the strike point? His awesome mind has already gone to the heart of the matter. Perhaps the mark you are about to strike is a mark of restoration: A young woman, bruised and battered, broken by life, has crumbled under the weight of years of hopelessness. Her tormentors are many, but our Archer has been watching over her... preparing you to fly to her in a time when her life shatters into a million pieces.

Think about it; God's eye is on her, His heart pounding as He draws you, His faithful arrow, back and breathes His love for her into the very depths of your being. His burden becomes the arrow's, His love removing all fear of flight.

What does the Word tell us?

> *God is love. When we take up permanent residence in a life of love, we live in God and God lives in us. This way, love has the run of the house...*
>
> 1 John 4:17

This place of final instruction becomes a place of deepening love and profound purpose. You must fully surrender and listen with every fiber of who you are. For a life hangs in the balance, and you are the arrow of rescue.

This is the point in which a great dichotomy occurs: You are tenderly broken by burden, yet strengthened by steel-enforced love. Though opposite in fleshly realms, strength and brokenness solidify and cement in the Spirit, infilling the arrow as it comes to lean against the mouth and ear of The Archer.

Though generally aligned in purpose as promoted, precision alignment now comes in the drawn back position. Final instructions are imparted in whispers. The arrow knows the minute adjustments necessary for strike. This is lock-in time. In this moment The Archer peers off into the distance (our Watchman God) and adjusts the bow accordingly.

Before we proceed, I feel I must take just a few minutes and share a word on spiritual alignment, for it is crucial to every single journey you will ever make.

Alignment: to get or fall into line, to be in or come into precise adjustment or correct relative position (I love that – correct relative position – for it is corrected relative to strike point).

Okay, on very practical terms, God always aligns you according to purpose. You will not be positioned according to gift or calling, or desire/talent. You will always be brought into line with purpose. For example: If God is going to use you in a specific body, there will be (if we submit, attend and listen) an aligning of your vision with the purpose and vision of the head of the body.

Alignment with purpose.

This is one reason that so many lone ranger arrows fall to the ground and are never seen again - they have nothing with which to align, and therefore never come under the commanded blessing; the oil does not flow over their lives.

Some do not want to hear that. Some can never settle the truth that they will flow and function best under a head, but it is true whether accepted or not. Alignment must take place in order for anointing to flow over and be rubbed into you.

Proper alignment opens your mantle to the blessings of unity. Can I tell you that when the oil of anointing and commanded blessing comes to the house in which you serve (or should be serving), it will pour first onto the head, then onto the collar, and then to the skirts?

> *How wonderful, how beautiful, when brothers and sisters get along! It's like costly anointing oil flowing down head and beard, flowing down Aaron's beard, flowing down the collar of his priestly robes. It's like the dew on Mount Hermon flowing down the slopes of Zion. Yes, that's where God commands the blessing, ordains eternal life.*
>
> Psalm 133:1-3

Oil flows from the head down, and in order to come under that flow, you must be spiritually aligned with your spiritual head. Will God pour over you individually? Absolutely; but it will be nothing like this. You see, there is a corporate anointing, a body vision, that when anointed and poured over, shakes nations and fells principalities. Operating alone, you set only a thousand to flight, but adding even one in agreement multiplies the flight exponentially. Corporate anointing leaves individual anointing running in the dust far behind. Massive oil is needed to anoint a corporation. I want oil like that!

Oh, do you understand, if you are one of those that refuses to align with the vision of the head; the purpose of authority, oil can come into the house, spilling over the head, down the beard, over the collar and onto the robes, and you will never even know it has happened? Scoffers, those sowing discord and maligning the head under which God has placed them, will deny the existence of anointing for they were never aligned to the blessing. When you have removed yourself so far from the covering, the only way you will touch the oil is if you move in repentance (in spirit) toward the head.

Please, if you have struggled with authority, go back and re-read the last paragraph. Get this before you move forward. This truth is pivotal to your spiritual health and prosperity.

Oh friend, you come into alignment through repentance, and through praying for your pastors, your leaders, those whom He has placed in spiritual authority over you. You want oil to flow through your church? Pray for your pastor. Cover him/her in prayer. Fast, intercede, support. Ask the Father to pour out an anointing that would absolutely drench him. Prayer alignment demands prayers offered for your head. If you are not praying for your pastor, how could you possibly think you have a right to complain and dissect his or her leadership?

Faithful prayer is the only thing that gives you a valid voice. If you are praying (I mean, truly praying) for your leadership and still have issues, then by all means, go to them and share your heart... not your opinions.

In the world, we understand that if we do not vote we truly have no right to complain about elected leaders. In the Spirit, we must understand that our prayers for the strengthening, wisdom and anointing of our head give us the right to speak out – to them, and them alone.

Are you aligned in purpose with those whom God has placed over you?

Now please listen to me. This form of alignment comes in the phase of promotion. Every place of promotion will demand a submission of some sorts. Submission will take you higher. Does that make sense to you? I cannot move into my next position until I have submitted fully in this one. So, stay with me just a moment, every promotion must come through submitting and aligning with the head of that level, for you cannot excel and move up through the ranks to stand in a position of leadership over that for which you have no vision.

In other words, if my pastor's vision is evangelism, I cannot be promoted in responsibility over evangelistic teams if I have not aligned myself to his vision. How can I be in authority and walk in fruitfulness over something I have no vision for? The same principle applies to those who receive promotion in the world. They must align themselves with the vision of the corporation. It is an absolute must for passionate presentation and effective dispensation of the message. Bottom line: You have to believe in why you are doing what you are doing in order to ever do it with excellence and complete conviction (convincing force). Everything else is just going through the motions.

So, my friend, as general alignment of vision takes place, you are promoted – not visa versa. You gain vision before promotion. Then upon full alignment, we receive a fuller promotion, grander vision. And when our head hits the ceiling, he draws us back for final specific alignment.

I know it may not make sense to you, but please take a moment and say a prayer, asking God to show you where you are in regards to alignment with whatever authority He has placed in your life. Ask Him to open your heart to revelation and give you understanding regarding proper spiritual alignment. It will make a world of difference in every flight you will ever take - and perhaps in whether or not you ever actually take flight.

When you are pulled or drawn back, there may be a perceived losing of ground; you may even feel like you are being punished or disciplined. Still, you will know deep on the inside that you have not lost ground because everything in you is still anticipatory of the next move. Oh, this is a hard but exciting place to be.

On the surface (in the earth/flesh realm), this position may manifest as having to lay down something once held precious. God may take you out of a much-loved position, or ask you to step away from relationships that distract. One of the harder things to deal with is the feeling that you have lost the favor of those over you. Do not fret. Do not get anxious and try to fix what is not broken. This is simply God's way of showing the arrow that it is His favor alone that is needed.

Another way this positioning may manifest is in an intensifying of the call to prayer and study of the Word. You may feel compelled to draw in close, and find yourself longing for a word from His lips. You hunger, and you feel as if something has been taken away, but the truth is, He has simply cleared your schedule for flight.

Several years ago, I went through a period of time when I felt like God was pulling out all of my props. (I cannot help but imagine the small sapling tree staked round about by pegs and ropes.) One by one He began to un-stake me. I thought He was weakening my position, leaving me subject to the elements, when in fact, with the removal of each stake came the need to strengthen by degree, leaving me not weakened, but unbound. Huge difference. When God removes our props and ropes it is not for the sake of vulnerability, but for the sake of full freedom.

Think about it, dear one - in the drawn-back position, the arrow is nearer to the ear and mouth of The Archer than they have ever been. You have His ear - and He has yours. He speaks in whispers that reverberate through you.

You have lost nothing, my friend! Indeed, you have gained intimate access to the ear and touch of The Archer.

In one (personally) earth-shattering instance, when pulled back, I had to lay down a class I loved, a position in the worship team, heading up a particular ministry I loved - pretty much everything I had counted on. But these were areas and positions He was promoting me through. The keyword being *through*, for it implies continual motion which allows you to move out of and beyond the other side of something. We move through promotion into position.

Ah, Jesus!

Those things He used at one time as lifting tools (places, services, positional responsibilities) are no longer needed, for you are no longer being lifted (promoted into position), you are being aligned. Alignment requires stillness on the part of the arrow. The arrow moves only by the hand of The Archer. The only thing the arrow need do is submit to His hand, and draw near the breath of The Archer.

Can you feel breath if you are running through chaotic winds? No, it is a small and intimate life force that flows over the arrow in moments of silence and stillness. Distracted, busy, encumbered, staked down and tied up, you will never move into the intimacy of the breath: that place where you sense God in every fiber of your being; where you are tightly strung, yet fully at peace; impatient, yet completely content in the waiting; excited, yet totally, somberly still.

Alone in the hand of The Archer, pulled back from everything and everyone, the world stops its frenetic dance as you are captured by the pulse which pounds its heady rhythm through His skilled fingertips.

Now comes sweet instruction. It may sound something like this:

When I release you, Daughter, you must carry this portion of love to the small one. Tell her to lift her head. Tell her that I am with her. Be led by compassion as you deal with her. Do not become weary as you move in close to her. She is going to try and send you away and make you turn your back on her. It is what she expects. She does not want to be hurt again by anyone or anything. She will not let you in willingly, but I want you to keep going back, faithfully administering my love to her. Meet her needs in this moment; let her talk as you bind her wounds with truth.

I know, some are saying, "Well, God does not get that specific with me." Sure He does. Everything I just said can be found in the Word:

This is how we know who the children of God are and who the children of the devil are: Anyone who does not do what is right is not a child of God; nor is anyone who does not love his brother. This is the message you heard from the beginning: We should love one another.

1 John 3:10-11 (NIV)

And when Jesus went out He saw a great multitude; and He was moved with compassion for them, and healed their sick.

Matthew 14:14 (NKJ)

So I say to you, ask and keep on asking and it shall be given you; seek and keep on seeking and you shall find; knock and keep on knocking and the door shall be opened to you.

Luke 11:9 (AMP)

And let our people also learn to maintain good works, to meet urgent needs, that they may not be unfruitful.

Titus 3:14 (NKJ)

It is all right there in the Word; love them, be persistent, be compassionate and meet their needs whenever you can. Final alignment; completed instruction. We just need to attend to His Word.

In the drawn-back position, His whispers may sound like words of encouragement, words and promises on which to stand, scriptural reminders, resurfacing of memories of past victories, gratitude or deliverance. When you are drawn back and rest this close to Him, His very fragrance will trigger truths about Him you had long forgotten. Like a wife's unconscious seeking of familiar aftershave on her husband's work shirt or winter coat, our faces are drawn into His fragrance, and we revel in all that is invoked in that moment. Ah, and when we leave that place we carry His fragrance deeply within our hearts.

When an archer brings an arrow up and back, it takes tremendous strength to pull back the bow. Having tried to do this myself, I am amazed at the ease with which my husband masters this thing. Once in place, fully drawn back, the strength of The Archer is completely engaged in the restraint of the arrow, while His intellect and vision are engaged in the positioning and alignment. He knows that if He releases the arrow before final alignment, it is going to miss the mark, and could possibly bring great harm to whatever is close - person, place or thing. The arm of The Archer remains taut and in full control for the safety of the arrow and all concerned. Yes, there is impetus behind the arrow. It will fly if released at this point. It just will not fly where it was intended to fly.

My point? When you feel the strength of The Archer drawing you back, do not rush your release, my friend.

Though you think you know, you may not. Though you might have an idea, you cannot be certain. Assurance and deep knowing come only in the breath moments. If you miss those, my friend, you may not find the stillness needed for final instruction, and you just might miss the mark.

You do not want to come this far and miss it. I know it can feel overwhelming. So many things are happening to you in this time, but you still feel inert; you see the strike point and long to take flight, yet you bask in the intimacy of the moment. I cannot help but believe this is a bit of what Paul was feeling when he wrote:

For to me, to live is Christ and to die is gain. If I am to go on living in the body, this will mean fruitful labor for me. Yet what shall I choose? I do not know! I am torn between the two: I desire to depart and be with Christ, which is better by far; but it is more necessary for you that I remain in the body. Convinced of this, I know that I will remain, and I will continue with all of you for your progress and joy in the faith, so that through my being with you again your joy in Christ Jesus will overflow on account of me.

Philippians 1:21-26 (NIV)

Stay or go? There is joy in both, but obedience is found in only one.

When God draws you back into close contact with Him, then restrains you in that position, friend, you are in the greatest and most intense phase of preparation you will experience. When you come into this phase, let Him speak. Listen!

In many of the phases you are a doer, but during these moments you must simply *be*. Allow quiet to infuse you. Settle into a place of soul peace. Keep a pen close, dear one, for when you quietly wait upon Him, attending to His Word, He will speak. Write down thoughts, impressions, prayers, dreams and scriptures. Be keen in the Spirit regarding any instruction given by those over you in the faith. After a time, you will begin to get a larger picture of your purposes; your vision increases in depth. Once things begin to clarify, you can know that release is coming. Let everything fit His hand, all impetus being gained through His strength alone.

You are probably in this stage if:

> You are experiencing a deep calm and stillness.
> You feel restrained yet powerful.
> You can see the vision so much more clearly than before.

You are no longer sensing upward motion.

God is speaking to you about the details in His Word.

You are suddenly unencumbered by strictures and old positions.

You have a new (and perhaps daunting) sense of freedom.

There is a new intensity to all that you are feeling and sensing in the Spirit.

You know He is breath-close, for you feel more alive than ever before.

Your love walk has increased and expanded far beyond the reaches of the quiver into the masses.

Ah, blessed arrow, stay upon the rest, be held within the confines of instruction, for soon enough His restrained power will be unleashed, and you will find yourself piercing the dark night, bringing light and illumination to the spirit skies, as you, fair-feathered one, are finally and completely...

Released!

Released

You own the cosmos - you made everything in it, everything from atom to archangel. You positioned the North and South Poles; the mountains Tabor and Hermon sing duets to you. With your well-muscled arm and your grip of steel - nobody trifles with you! The Right and Justice are the roots of your rule; Love and Truth are its fruits. Blessed are the people who know the passwords of praise, who shout on parade in the bright presence of God. Delighted, they dance all day long; they know who you are, what you do - they can't keep it quiet! Your vibrant beauty has gotten inside us - you've been so good to us! We're walking on air! All we are and have we owe to God, Holy God of Israel, our King!

Psalm 89:11-18

Oh, my goodness! Can you believe we are actually here, standing on the precipice of full release? What can possibly compare to this stirring? Everything in you is charged, anticipatory, longing, taut and excruciatingly awake. This is no pins and needles kind of feeling, but a deep river kind of moment. Gratitude washes through you as your journey to this point clarifies and congeals. Thankfulness marries purpose and the union infuses your soul. Your emotions line up with your deepest hopes as destiny calls your name. Waiting, suspended in time, the strength of The Archer restrains you for incandescent seconds. His final whisper rocks you: *Fly true, Beloved.*

You rest in a place of hair-trigger alertness. You know it is coming. Suddenly, the *rest* drops from beneath you, and you are suspended for the briefest moment, before you kiss the wind full-face.

No rest to seek ease upon, nor nocking point to grab onto, The Archer's strong right arm holds its position, as His fingers open. The winds cradle you; surrounded, propelled, drawn, your razor point rips through the elements, dividing space, creating an invisible pathway for the purposes of The Archer. The mist clears, light penetrates all shadows and the target appears directly before you. Going deep, a war cry breaks forth from the depths of the arrow, as disciplined preparation meets divine opportunity and the arrow strikes the deep red center; a joining which resounds through earth and heavens. Like the sound of Peter dropping his nets to follow Christ, this sound is unlike all other, yet completely known by those with ears to hear.

The earth trembles.

God rules: there's something to shout over! On the double, mainlands and islands - celebrate! Bright clouds and storm clouds circle 'round him; Right and justice anchor his rule. Fire blazes out before him, Flaming high up the craggy mountains. His lightnings light up the world; Earth, wide-eyed, trembles in fear. The mountains take one look at God And melt, melt like wax before earth's Lord. The heavens announce that he'll set everything right, And everyone will see it happen - glorious! All who serve handcrafted gods will be sorry - And they were so proud of their ragamuffin gods! On your knees, all you gods -

worship him! And Zion, you listen and take heart! Daughters of Zion, sing your hearts out: God has done it all, has set everything right.

Psalm 97:1-8

Rejoice, dear arrow, rejoice! You have flown true, you have taken a step you have never taken before; facing your fear and completing the work required to finally soar. Oh, my friend, it literally brings tears to my eyes. What a blessed moment to be fully utilized by God, to have your hopes and dreams realized!

How long have you waited for this moment? How long have you dreamed of flying in fullness, basking in purpose? Understand, I am not talking about fame and fortune here. I am talking about finally knowing that you are absolutely in the center of His will for you, using your gifts, your talents, your abilities to serve Him in faithfulness as never before.

What a wonderful thing it is that the God of the Universe uses human beings to rock eternal places. He, in His omniscience, uses the weakness of flesh to display the strength of the Spirit. To know that He has someone specifically designed and destined to speak into each individual life just blows me away. To know that He has placed words of comfort in my spirit for the changing of someone else's life truly humbles me. How horrid it would be for me to withhold them, never offering solace to the one who needed it.

In all of this, do you begin to understand how important it is for us to discipline our lives to the training necessary to effectively strike the marks God has designated for us to strike? Do you see that self-preoccupation is the enemy of flight?

We have been so busy being repeatedly healed from past wounds, we haven't had time to bring healing to others. How many times must we pull off a scab and weep over wounds that should have healed long ago? Dear One, we were created to fly to the aid of others, yet we continually feel the need to aid ourselves. This should not be. We no longer have time for "It's all about me" seminars and classes. We are arrows in His hand, and our strike point does not lie within ourselves.

The strongest pull in this section, I believe, lies in the understanding of your purpose in release. You must be committed to your *why*, for purpose is not found in your flight, but in *why* you are being sent.

There was a point in my life when I had been calling out to the Lord for a very long time, asking Him to "release me" into the ministry that I felt called to. I knew a drawing toward teaching and writing, but doors just would not open for me. I can speculate on why the doors would not open. Perhaps (she said sarcastically) it was my complete lack of discipline to study, or the emotional inconsistencies of my walk.

Then again, it could have been the fact that I had a family to care for and children to raise – my first calling and priority. You might throw failure to submit, bad attitude and rebellion into the mix... if you were so inclined. Add to that the fact that I was unprepared and it was not my season, and it is pretty easy to see (in retrospect) why my "International Ministry" remained in my living room.

The biggest deal-breaker, however, was found in the truth that I had no idea what my *why* was. I did not have a reason for being sent out. God could not release me. I was dangerous, a threat to myself and the Body of Christ. If you do not have a *God-why*, you will inevitably get a *world-why*.

Friend, good intentions, even great intentions, morph very easily into selfish motive when unrestrained and unguarded by God-whys.

Let me tell you a little secret here: I have discovered something quite interesting about this God we serve. He often requires you to perform as if released even before you truly are, for the sole purpose of clarifying your why.

Let me explain. As I sought the Lord (a.k.a. begged and pleaded) for release, He began to speak to my heart in the night and woo me away from my warm bed. He began to test me to see if I would get up with Him and seek Him in the night watches. Did I pass? Sometimes. Other times I would simply roll over and pretend I hadn't heard Him. I did not control my flesh, making it rouse from slumber. In doing this small thing, He was making me keenly aware of the lack of discipline in my life. He would draw me to the Word, but distraction would win the day. I would take off with friends or follow my own desires. He would send someone along who needed help or comfort and I would become frustrated by their need.

In the end I found that He was masterfully revealing my heart, exposing my why to me.

He then began to wake me up in the night with a single solitary word; one simple expository question. A million nuances and inquiries in one eternity exposing syllable: "Why?"

I knew in my heart He was asking why I wanted to be "sent out". He didn't have to pose anything other than the why. Time after time the question awakened me in midnight conference, and time after time I struggled and could find no answer... not a good, honest one, anyway. It was so frustrating, this constant trying to get to the core, to the center, to the purposeful why!

I argued with the darkness. I mean, *Doesn't it matter that I want to go out on Your behalf... to be used by You, God?*

In the final analysis, not really. He did not need me to simply go for the sake of going. Many are willing to travel. Many are willing to speak. Many are willing to hold a microphone. But those who have an actual reason for doing so are few and far between. Few have found their why. Few have found their purpose. Few have found their spirit's message.

He didn't need another random arrow. He was looking for precision.

Enter paragon of spiritual maturity...

What's with all these questions? Fine. Great! You don't want me to go, I won't go! You want to make things difficult? Well, I can just do what I'm doing for the rest of my life. I do not need to do anything in order to be fulfilled. I'm happy. I have three children who need me, a husband who thinks I'm great. My friends like me and I do not have to "do" anything to make my life feel complete. My life is just fine the way it is, thank you very much!

Come again, the midnight why.

Oh, God, not again! I do not have the answer! Why do you keep asking me for an answer I do not have?

"Because you need this answer. Because I need you to look deeper. I need you to know the answer."

Honestly, I cried so much during this time of my life, it was just ridiculous. Though everything on the surface was great, the hunger in my spirit was overwhelming. I was desperate to find Him in a deeper, more meaningful way. I needed to know Him - not in the way I had known Him before, but the way I had to know Him in order to move into what I felt Him moving me into.

Oh, but I was so lazy. The war between my flesh and my spirit was great. I was so frustrated with myself, the people around me, and most especially at God for not giving me the answer to His question. I mean, after all, He knew that my release hanged on His *why*.

There is a vast difference between our why and His, and within that chasm lays huge potential for defeat and destruction of purpose. God knows that. He forces the issue of why-establishment so you will have to dig deep, plant firm and keep your legs strong underneath you.

I had no choice. I had to dig into the Word. I knew it would birth the truth in me. Only the Word can bring this kind of answer to the surface of your spirit-man.

Oh, let me tell you, I studied! I was crazy-hungry for the answers I knew I would find there. He drew me (through hunger) into passionate and relentless study. He had me study as one undergoing an exam. He made me (through seeking answers) write papers and delve into His Word on a consistent and substantial basis. He schooled me. He trained me. He placed me in situations where I had no choice but to walk in discipline or fall on my face for lack of it.

Finally, after many months of digging, crying, teaching, studying, He chose a nondescript, starry midnight and awakened me once again with His one whispered syllable.

"Why?"

This time, however, the answer flowed from my heart, bypassing conscious thought and tumbled from my lips encased in a river of Truth. *Because I love them...* I offered my breath and beating heart into His waiting grasp. *Because I love them...* the rhythm of Christ's nature coursed through my veins. Tears began to flow down my face.

"Yes," He answered, *"Because you love them."*

My life changed in that moment.

I literally sobbed to the point of not being able to breathe. My heart felt as if it became liquid within my chest.

Everything crystallized within my spirit. I believe in that night-watch He infused my spirit with a love unlike anything I had ever experienced before. It was a love borne of compassion and mercy, understanding and comfort. It was deep and profound - and it changed me. I could no longer live the way I had been living. I could not settle for surface service, but plunged with great abandon into faithful purpose. It was overwhelming in its magnitude and richness. A love for His children rocked my world. I cannot tell you in human words how my life has been altered since that moment.

He released me... to love. That release has birthed every release since that point.

Dear arrow, as uncomplicated as it seems, this is deep and divine revelation. Open your heart to understanding. Can I prophesy into your life the powerful truth of this one thing? Love will be your release, for love must always be your why. It sounds so simple, and I know we have discussed this before, but you must always come back to *why*.

I remember so clearly the weeks following this outpouring of love in my life. I would come into service and just stand in the back of the room, look at the people and weep. As I looked over the congregation, and into the faces of the hurting, I would long to comfort them, to encourage them, to hold them in my heart. It was overwhelming in intensity and clarity. There was actually a level of love I had never even come close to touching in this flesh. It was huge in its ramifications! I finally caught the smallest glimpse of the magnanimous heart of God, The Archer.

I finally got it.

One day the Lord reminded me of His Own heart-cry.

> *O Jerusalem, Jerusalem, you who kill the prophets and stone those sent to you, how often I have longed to gather your children together, as a hen gathers her chicks under her wings, but you were not willing.*
> Matthew 23:37 (NIV)

You see, in order for God to use you, to release you fully, there must be a longing in your heart to gather the lost and the broken, to cover them and bring them into safety. Having an understanding of and moving into a sympathetic vibration with Jesus' heart as He overlooked Jerusalem, is pivotal to your release. He saw them for what they were -

132

"those who kill the prophets" - yet longed to draw them to Himself and protect them.

Can we have that kind of love, that kind of heart? Can we see the reality of the situation, the frailties and failures of humanity at its worst, but know the hope of God's redemptive love? Can we look at broken lives, sin-filled hearts and bitter facts, and find the truth of desired restoration? Will we see with God-eyes, love with God-love and serve with God-purpose? This, beloved, is the core truth. This reveals the depth of our *why*.

You can remain in the drawn back position for a long time awaiting this whispered truth: *I will release you to fly when love compels you go.* That is the trigger-release. You love, and "Surprise!" the trigger releases.

Archery 101

The "correct" way to use a release device is with a "surprise break." By this, you bring the bow to the target, and when you are happy with the sight picture, you initiate a shot that will happen over the next few seconds. However, you do not know exactly when the arrow will leave, so the shot is a surprise.

Isn't that just the way it goes? You think you are prepared for flight, but when the moment actually arrives you are still so surprised. Your surroundings seem a bit blurry as you hit your stride.

Hah! Sent without warning, you had no time to get scared!

I love when He does that. He offered no descending countdown; no *3, 2, 1... fly!* He did not do this so that you would be unprepared, but that you would be unguarded.

Flight is a vulnerable thing for the arrow. Full trust must remain in The Archer. His skill is the arrow's salvation. Unguarded, fully abandoned in service, you will strike marks you could not possibly strike when flying with reservation.

What do I mean? Well, in simplest terms, your pain often ministers more deeply than your victory. Your failure speaks to more than your success. The things we hide and long to distance ourselves from are the very things that give us access to the hearts of others. Though I rejoice in your accomplishments, I am moved by your struggle. While your breakthrough moments inspire me, the fight to get there connects with my humanity.

Surprise release provides a venue for flight without time to put up our walls. We move forward and go face-first into the target area tender, broken and accessible; more powerful than ever in our complete vulnerability. Not quite what we imagine when we think of striking the mark, huh? We think precision, when in fact we may feel random in the flesh. We may feel scattered and disjointed, and perhaps even unready. But that merely serves to keep us dependent upon The Archer.

Understand, Fierce Arrow, though we are never unprepared after having gone through the instruction processes of the arrow, we may still feel unqualified. We may have great desire coupled with flashes of uncertainty. *God, are you sure I can do this? Have you seen the way I _____ (you fill in the blank). You know I cannot speak like her.*

> *Moses raised another objection to God: "Master, please, I don't talk well. I've never been good with words, neither before nor after you spoke to me. I stutter and stammer." God said, "And who do you think made the human mouth?*

And who makes some mute, some deaf, some sighted, some blind? Isn't it I, God? So, get going. I'll be right there with you – with your mouth! I'll be right there to teach you what to say." He said, "Oh, Master, please! Send somebody else!"

Exodus 4:10-13

Can I offer you a bit of a heads-up here? Right before your release you will very likely experience an onslaught of personal uncertainty. Let this become a signpost in your journey; standing between you and every door of opportunity is a spirit of fear sent to stop you in your tracks. When fear/anxiety raises its head, look for the door.

Have you ever stood on the very threshold of release only to back down because of fear? Have you been in this place (where you now stand) before? Friend, fear backs down only at the eternal love and authority found in God's Word.

You can pray pretty prayers and sound extremely righteous, but if the words you use are your own, the enemy remains undaunted. The power of God's Word defeats your greatest fears. You can shout, rebuke, fuss and complain all you want, but only God's Truth will deliver you.

Dear friends, let us love one another, for love comes from God. Everyone who loves has been born of God and knows God. Whoever does not love does not know God, because God is love. This is how God showed his love among us: He sent his one and only Son into the world that we might live through him. This is love: not that we loved God, but that he loved us and sent his Son as an atoning sacrifice for our sins. Dear friends, since God so loved us, we also ought to love one another. No one has ever seen God; but if we love one another, God lives in us and his love is made complete in us.

We know that we live in him and he in us, because he has given us of his Spirit. And we have seen and testify that the Father has sent his Son to be the Savior of the world. If anyone acknowledges that Jesus is the Son of God, God lives in him and he in God. And so we know and rely on the love God has for us. God is love. Whoever lives in love lives in God, and God in him. In this way, love is made complete among us so that we will have confidence on the day of judgment, because in this world we are like him. There is no fear in love. But perfect love drives out fear, because fear has to do with punishment. The one who fears is not made perfect in love.

We love because he first loved us. If anyone says, "I love God," yet hates his brother, he is a liar. For anyone who does not love his brother, whom he has seen, cannot love God, whom he has not seen. And he has given us this command: Whoever loves God must also love his brother.

I John 4:7-21 (NIV)

With deep and true love as the motivator, you can move beyond your fears into full release.

One day my husband, Hal, and I were sitting on our front porch, having a glass of tea with a couple of friends, My daughter, Kaitlen, and one of her friends had decided to walk our new puppy, Skootch, and had placed her on her leash. They were going to walk up to the cul-de-sac (a mere two houses to out left and in plain sight of our porch). With a clear line of vision, we had no reason to be concerned or fearful for her safety. So, we relaxed and talked with our friends. Then, without warning, came the kind of scream no parent wants to hear.

"Mama!"

The adults turned in unison, to see Kaitlen, her friend, and our little white puppy running for all they were worth. Behind them, literally on their little heels, was a huge black Chow with teeth bared. Unrestrained, no leash, no fence, it was on the attack. Fear filled their little faces, and their legs just could not move fast enough.

In that moment, many things happened at once. My friend, Christine, began praying out loud (I love her so!), calling on God. My husband, then 50 years of age, stood, jumped forward, legs clearing the porch banister and landed in full stride heading toward the girls. My friend's husband followed, and I ran down the steps behind. Like a freeze frame moment, the dog lunged forward, grabbing the first thing it could get its teeth into - our puppy. It bit into the pup's back and lifted it from the ground, shaking it furiously.

Hal reached the chow about the time the girls made it into Christine's arms. She held them against her chest, hiding their faces from the violent sight, offering a mother's comfort. At that same time, Hal reached out with both hands and lifted the chow off the ground by the fur on its back, shaking the 60 pound animal until it released our puppy. Our pup fell crying and wounded to the ground. Hal launched the chow on a flight all its own.

General chaos ensued, but we will not delve into the aftermath. I will simply say the puppy survived after extensive surgery, and the girls would eventually overcome their fears and the images planted in their minds. Though traumatic, God had covered the moment.

God has used this moment many times to reiterate to me the power of His love. You see, in that desperate moment, perfect love truly cast out all fear. There could have been a whole pack of dogs and my husband would have still leapt that banister and ran into the battle. His love for his baby girl demanded a response, and fear did not enter into the equation. He did not sit and ponder, *should I or shouldn't I?* He did not weigh his options or make a few phone calls for opinions. Love had to act. It was who he was. It wasn't a gifting issue, or even a calling. It was instinctual, primal, base-line love. In that moment on my porch, love destroyed all barriers.

My husband did not see the fierceness of the dog, but his love for his daughter. His love for her made him fearless. There was not even a split second when he considered the bite of the dog. He was in rescue mode. He had a strike point, and the motivator was love.

His was a surprise release, one unexpected yet fully prepared for. Love had equipped him with everything he needed in that moment. Fear was irrelevant.

The same must be true for you, my friend. In your moment of release, all fear barriers must fall at the feet of love. You must fly because love demands it.

Trust me. When God releases you, in a moment of surprise or one that comes with warning, the love within you will equip you with all that you need. It will move you beyond all of the barriers. It will demand a response - one that is instinctive and does not even require measured thought.

God-love changes your instincts and mutes the voice of fear. But, without love, you are not ready, and fear's taunts will stop you every time.

Now, back to your moment.

Released in love, you now fly, and why you are going has become quite evident. Ah, friend, wherever The Archer has sent you, fly true. Remember to release all glory. Sew generously into the lives of all you come in contact with. Complete your work with excellence and diligence. Stay in it until God takes you out of it. Do not be in a hurry to move on, but stay and be of maximum effect. When you become weary, pray and encourage yourself in the faith. When you feel frustrated, draw from the wells of love. When you long for the warmth and safety of the quiver, draw your strength from God. Keep putting one foot in front of the other, one prayer on top of the other, until you arrive at the other side of this destined point. You will go strike true.

Stuck dead-center in a bright red target, striking your mark might feel like the end point of your journey, but it is not. It is just the beginning. God is not the only one taking aim.

What you thought would be the victory point has now become your battleground. You head into this field to retrieve the wounded, the broken, the disoriented, the maimed and the battle weary. Here, you are called to carry their weight, and bring them to safety, or toward peace and rest.

What? I just wanted to lead worship for thousands and speak to nations!

Again, I ask you why? Why do you want to do those things? Is it for His glory or for your own? Is it because you have a need or because they do?

Ah, Sweet Arrow, you must never forget, the arrow's creation was that of a weapon. You are a weapon formed and forged in fire for use in battle. Though some eventually hang on walls and in museums, they were never created for such things. An arrow is intended for the complete and total destruction of an enemy. Period.

If your strike point is nations, you will face the enemy of nations. In this great call, know that your shoulders will bare much, and only love can send you flying over banisters of this height and magnitude. If your strike point, your mark, is worship and a Levite call, know that the Levites faced the armies before the soldiers ever stood face to face with them.

You are a Warrior's weapon. You must never lose sight of that truth. We fight for King and Kingdom. Every arrow that strikes its mark effectively, and returns to the King that which belongs to Him.

Though you may feel small and insignificant, your Archer is skilled and mighty. Together, we storm the battlefields of the Lord!

> *When the angel of the LORD appeared to Gideon, he said, "The LORD is with you, mighty warrior."*
> *The LORD turned to him and said, "Go in the strength you have and save Israel out of Midian's hand. Am I not sending you?"*
> *"But Lord, "Gideon asked, "how can I save Israel? My clan is the weakest in Manasseh, and I am the least in my*

> *family." The LORD answered, "I will be with you, and you will strike down all the Midianites together."*
>
> Judges 6:12-16 (NIV)

You may be in this phase if:

You sense the beat of battle drums within your spirit.
You know the taste of fear, but the call of love.
You feel the "rest" falling away.
God's close whisper is exchanged for a war cry.
You finally have your why.
You are very tender toward the flock.
You are completely fed up with weak and watery Christianity.
You see the wounded and broken with new eyes.
You have stopped waiting for someone else to go to the rescue.
You are completely convinced your God has your back.

In this divine moment, know that the battle belongs to the Lord, but you may be called to fight, to carry love without limit, to serve without reservation, to fly without restraint.

Be released, in the name of Jesus.

The Good Arrow

Then I'll send off my servant, "Go find the arrows."
1 Samuel 20:21

Step down out of heaven, God; ignite volcanoes in the hearts of the mountains. Hurl your lightnings in every direction; shoot your arrows this way and that. Reach all the way from sky to sea.
Psalm 144:5

Here we are, my dear and precious arrows, our time of instruction now resting in sands behind well-worn sandals. Our journey sweetening and fermenting with time, we find within ourselves the birthing of that which is far richer than any worldly wine; spiritual maturity.

We ponder His goodness upon the path and we swell in gratitude. Small and momentary flashes of revelation still bring the involuntary shiver as God-truth seeps through fragments of unenlightened sleeping flesh, and deep calls to deep – awakening and stirring dormant passion.

Beloved, you are changed. From glory to glory He has taken you through. Never will you be the same. You have found God in a new and profound way. He is The Master Archer, and you are an arrow in His hand.

You have vision. You have newfound purpose and burgeoning hope. Breath has filled your lungs. Everything is different now. You finally know that God can and will use you. And you have settled your why.

Oh God, how I love You! How precious and weighty your thoughts unto me. Lover of my soul, I adore You! This journey from choice to soaring has come through your hand alone. It is just too much for me to comprehend.

You have been through so much now. Can we just walk this out for a moment? Mental pictures of the journey have been logged and dated, and I simply must pull a few of them out and shed a tear or two.

CHOSEN

> *So, chosen by God for this new life of love, dress in the wardrobe God picked out for you: compassion, kindness, humility, quiet strength, discipline. Be even-tempered, content with second place, quick to forgive an offense. Forgive as quickly and completely as the Master forgave you. And regardless of what else you put on, wear love. It's your basic, all-purpose garment. Never be without it.*
>
> Colossians 3:12-14

In the beginning we wondered if God could ever use us. Bruised and bloodied, mired in sin, feeling unworthy and unwanted, we knew all of the reasons why He could not and should not use us. Having flown one too many flights for the enemy, we were lost in fields of shame and reproach. Abandoned, covered in layers of dirt and filth, we had no hope of retrieval. We grew accustomed to being hidden and bound by silence... until He, our Archer, walked the field in search of one that was lost.

Oh, the moment His feet touched the dust from which we came, the earth resounded, shaking loose the soil of our surroundings. One foot in front of the other, He sought us out, coming toward us with great purpose. For, you see, He had never truly lost sight of us. Never, Dear One! In that field, in that moment, Blessed Arrow, He stooped down, picked you up, dusted you off and *chose* you.

He did not wonder what He would do with you, or what purpose you might serve. Oh, do you understand? He already knew you, already had a plan and already knew the number of your days. He came to get you because it was time for you to step into the destiny He had for you. Love demanded He move. For we all know arrows must have an Archer to accomplish anything.

He sought you. He retrieved you. He made you His own. He chose you.

> *I've looked over the field and chosen you for this work.*
>
> Haggai 2:23

Chosen, He then began the work of preparation, for our Archer has never been caught unprepared. His skill is unparalleled; the tools in His hand must therefore, be matchless. So He shapes, molds and tests.

TESTED FOR TRUE

> *But he knows where I am and what I've done. He can cross-examine me all he wants, and I'll pass the test with honors. I've followed him closely, my feet in his footprints, not once swerving from his way.*
>
> Job 23:10-11

Oh, friend, do you remember the times of testing we have walked through? Can you look back and see that in all things He has been watching our flight? I would daresay that everyone who has touched this study has found themselves in times of testing, as The Archer awakened warrior arrows and stirred those long dormant. Like a limb which comes to life after repressed blood flow, the pain of a thousand nerve ending needles has moved us, reaffirming our discomfort at having God-potential; potential that we might actually one day be used to bring honor to the King.

Many of you have pulled up bootstraps and squared shoulders, saying to The Archer with every fiber of your being, "Bring it on!" Others, with fear and trepidation have stepped up and with tear-filled eyes whispered, "If You can use me, God... here I am."

Fully exposed, His examination has been thorough. Yet, through love, you were made strong enough to withstand close scrutiny. You understand its great necessity, the preparation it portends. The small flights, the little tests and trials have only served to strengthen your resolve, moving you forward in faith and purpose. Things that might have once thrown you a curve, now merely plant your feet with more certainty. Yes, you have determined that no matter what comes, you will be faithful; you will fly true.

Just the thought of this goodness, the benevolence of Christ, overwhelms me. Arrows, once ruled by fear of failure, have now through merciful test flights, come to realize that even if they miss it they are loved beyond measure. Their worth no longer tied up in their performance, they are now free to fly; trusting The Archer for the outcome. Type A personalities all over the world can now relax. God has your back. The battle is His, and the only way you can truly fail this test is if you refuse to take it.

Having been tested for true, you can rest for a bit… and you find yourself in a time of surrounding.

HIDDEN

Sharpen the arrows! Fill the quivers!

Jeremiah 51:11

During this time you probably found yourself longing to get away from all of these people. I find it so interesting that when God puts us in a safe place, the enemy tries to twist it and make us feel uncovered. What God intends as warmth and comfort, we begin to see as smothering repression.

In the beginning, our placement in the quiver almost felt like a punishment. Our thoughts had a tendency to stray to, "I must have done something wrong, because He is not using me like I thought He would." Instead of opening our hearts and spirits to those around us, we longed for fairer fields, microphones and platforms. We saw our potential as wasted among those who did not see God's gifting within us, when in truth, we were being called to see the greatness of the gift within them.

In the quiver, in the midst of the congregation, God began to do an unexpected work, one we thought had already been accomplished: He taught us about love. Oh, we thought we knew what love was, but we did not - not until He placed us right in the midst of those we sought to leave behind.

Why is it that we always assume the greater need is always far beyond our own doors, when sadly, the one sitting beside us every single Sunday, still weeps?

146

Yes, in the quiver, we became aware of needs outside of our own, experienced heartbreaks having nothing to do with our own little worlds, and devastating pains we would have once avoided like the plague. In the quiver, life became real. Family members died, children became sick, husbands left, and women mourned; the tears of the saints pierced the armor of our souls. In the awakening of the quiver, joys went deeper and songs took on new meaning. Laughter healed you and the linking of arms became a daily expectation. The workings of the quiver painted your soul in bold colors, and left your heart a bloody mess. Pierced, broken, yet somehow splendidly whole, love won the day, changing you irrevocably and forever.

Again, overwhelmed.

EXPOSED

The purity of silver and gold is tested by putting them in the fire;
The purity of human hearts is tested by giving them a little fame.

Proverbs 27:21

When The Archer reached into the quiver and singled you out, you longed to hold onto what you had come to know and retain your place in the fold. Yet, because of the work of love, you let go when you might have clung, for love compelled you go. Love now has the final word.

Flesh once screamed loudest, issuing its commands with selfish abandon, but no longer. A new voice rules you. A new purpose drives you. A new hope draws you. You are finally completely willing to move away from your preconceived notions of what it means to be used by God, and move into

His *whatever*. Once afraid of appearing weak or vulnerable, love has opened you up to a whole new revelation. You now know that it is only in your vulnerabilities that you are truly known.

Now, when The Archer brings you out into the open and puts you before the others, you no longer feel the need to hide behind smoke and mirrors. Your longing to appear strong and without flaw has been left far behind, for you have seen and experienced the power of love in the face of true need.

You think back to your moments in the quiver when your heart was filled with compassion for those who had need of you; how your heart split wide open as you poured into them all that God had given you. You find that you are now willing to stand before others with exposed heart and apparent need. You have become vulnerable to man, yet stronger in Kingdom terms than you have ever been in your life. Your weakness has now become your greatest strength. Willing to be exposed in even your insecurities, God brings you up and out of the quiver. After being long hidden, the rush of this moment is palpable.

When God brings you out it is an awesome and humbling thing. Trust has now become your constant companion. Even when you do not understand everything that is going on around you, you can find peace in simply knowing He has you.

That first true exposure is unforgettable. When all eyes lock on you, the tendency is to present only the beautiful and the strong places, but exposure is exposure, and all is out in the open. It is almost funny, this dichotomy of emotion. On one hand you want to give a huge "Woohoo, I'm out!" while the other part of you – the part now accustomed to the warmth of the quiver – has an "Oh, Jesus! Put-me–back!" moment.

Still, once exposed, you move beautifully; fully reliant upon the hand that brought you out. Trusting, hoping for the best, you pray that your exposure brings Him glory, as you steel yourself against praise and judgment respectively. You move higher, still held within His grip. Catching the light in flashing beauty, what you radiate is Him. Never to be the source of glory, you become the reflection of all that He is. A mirror of His grandeur, you pour out His likeness, and all of the *oohs* and *aahs* flow back to the creator of Arrow flight... The Archer.

My prayer is that we would all be the truest reflection of His majesty. May we keep our lives clean and spotless so that there is nothing to distort His pure image when others seek to find His likeness in us.

> *God made the heavens - Royal splendor radiates from him,*
> *A powerful beauty sets him apart.*

Psalm 96:5

Oh, friend, in times of exposure may we all reflect the beautiful power that sets Him apart! Flying high, brought to the notice of others, our hearts were tested. A little fame revealed much – both good and bad – and in that moment of revelation, we found ourselves moving steadily toward our own reality; the truth of who we are both with and without The Archer. A mere arrow, our frailty and failure belies our humanity, as the God-awareness adds dimension and depth to our shallow lives. Soaring one moment, brought face to face with our humanity the next, we went facedown before Him... and we recognized greatness.

FACEDOWN

> *I sewed myself a shroud and wore it like a shirt; I lay facedown in the dirt. Now my face is blotched red from weeping; look at the dark shadows under my eyes,*
> *Even though I've never hurt a soul and my prayers are sincere!*
>
> Job 16:15-17

I know this place. You know this place. The chasm between humanity and divinity bids us swing low, facing our own composition on a staggeringly repetitive basis. It is in this place that we get a grip on His grandeur; our own limitations declaring His limitlessness.

How precious this journey into truth. For in this life we have been given, we have such great tendency to view ourselves unrealistically, either through shame's distortion, or the misshapen imagery of pride. In the light of these two funhouse mirrors, we are either far less than adequate, or inflated in our own estimations. Neither, my friend, is a true and accurate portrayal.

The glorious enlightenments of God revelation in facedown moments are the most life altering you will ever experience. In places of deepest humility, God shows you a side of yourself you have never known. At His feet, you find a lovely strength and completeness that would allow you to kneel forever before Him, and in that, He begins to lift you once again. A willingness and longing to stay at His feet fully displays your readiness to move beyond that place.

All of those times you cried and prayed for Him to send you out, to use you, have now become a part of who you *were*, as

who you *are* settles into a place of replete contentment at His feet. Willing to stay, He now bids you go.

I love that! I love a God Who does not act and look like we want or expect. I love that He shakes things up and turns left when we expect Him to make a right. He so tickles me! I often get this picture in my mind of Him smiling as we burst out in laughter at the unexpectedness of His next move. He absolutely captivates me. His thoughts and ways leave me shaking my head as my internal dialogue repeats, *Oh no, you did not just do that!* Truly, who has a God like this?

Truth and reality-of-self established, His hand began to raise us.

PROMOTED AND ALIGNED

> *When God, who is the best shepherd of all, comes out in the open with his rule, he'll see that you've done it right and commend you lavishly. And you who are younger must follow your leaders. But all of you, leaders and followers alike, are to be down to earth with each other, for – God has had it with the proud, But takes delight in just plain people. So be content with who you are, and don't put on airs. God's strong hand is on you; he'll promote you at the right time.*

> 1 Peter 5:4-6

God-reality nocking us upon the bowstring, we became stable and locked into place. Up, up and away from the feet, we found new purpose. We began to see things differently. Our line of sight quickly changing, we adjusted to the new positioning and allowed Him to do the work He needed to do in order to make the small and minute corrections that had to be made.

No longer struggling with self and image and the perception of others, we allowed Him to move us at will. Concern for the judgments of others a thing of the past; we truly do not care how we look in the raising, as long as we reflect Him. Moving up in realms of faithfulness, steadfastness, commitment, covenant and revelation, we became a weapon by increasing degree.

Once a me-arrow, longing for self-fulfillment and positioning, the instruction of the arrow has schooled you, morphing your purpose. Profoundly different in vision and calling, you rest in His hand through all positioning and promotion. You know it did not come because of you, and does not, therefore depend on you.

This is a truly good thing to know. It is all about Him. This is The Archer's battle, The Archer's field. He is in full and complete control and you are at rest in that knowledge.

Once the be-all-end-all, the world's positions are merely launching points now. Back pats and accolades rank right up there with gum wrappers and yesterday's newspaper. The need simply isn't there any longer, and for this we must become deeply grateful. Our motivators have changed, and accordingly, our ability to stay the course. Where once we might have become disheartened by lack of notice, we are unmoved by external motivators... or the lack thereof.

A big hallelujah has filled the heart of an unbound arrow! Locked, lifted, and aligned, we have found surety. Archer and Arrow move as one: He draws us back.

DRAWN BACK

He fills his hands with lightning

152

and commands it to strike its mark.

Job 36:32 (NIV)

Whispers, your reward; God-breath stirred you, as His Arm drew you back, moving you into intimate closeness with The Archer. An *Ahhhh, Jesus!* would be absolutely appropriate at this moment.

How far we have come in His hand. Every motion and emotion now flowing with purpose, we rest near His mouth and ear, as He speaks wise instruction and listens to the changed cry of our heart.

Hope, purpose, vision and mission clarify as He asks one question: *"Why?"* and from your deep well comes the answer: *"Only Love!"* The rest falls from beneath you, The Archer's fingers relax their grip upon the bowstring, as with heretofore unknown impetus, you find complete and total release.

RELEASED

His lightnings light up the world;
Earth, wide-eyed, trembles in fear.

Psalm 97:4

It may not have looked like you thought it would look; may not have been the destination you expected, but He released you; unleashing you, the earth trembled at His goodness.

I cannot speak further of your release, for to each it will be different and profound. To try and tell you what this phase will look like in your own life is beyond my human capabilities. I cannot tell you where He will send you and what your results will be.

Though I would love to paint you a picture of victory and exultation, your sending may appear in the form of tears and trial. If I were to expound upon palm branch inductions and rose petals in pathways, you might think yourself unsent when met with stones and jeers. To do this would discredit The Archer and His ability to send with accuracy and intent.

Simply know this: when He sends you, He sends with an endowment of power unequalled in strength, unbowed in purpose. The rhythm of His own heart will pound within your chest when His hand releases you. Listen for His rhythm. Know that He will be in the midst of you, no matter the destination.

Chosen, Tested, Hidden, Exposed, Facedown, Promoted, Aligned, Drawn Back and finally Released, you, Precious Arrow, now know The Archer as never before. All that you have learned and come to know is now a part of your lifeblood. From now until forever you will be an arrow in His hand. In this, you have one final commitment and covenant: You must worship.

The One Who has done all of this deserves your praise, is worthy of your honor. He is King and Lord of all, Master and Creator. Mighty Warrior and Commander of Angel Armies, all of our worship is due Him. Let your response be absolute awe. Let your song be His alone. If you exult, let it be in Him. If you weep, let your tears touch His feet. In your rising, acknowledge how you did so; in your sitting let His peace settle you.

God, our Master Archer strings His bow and nocks His arrows into place, and nations hold their breath in anticipation. Oh yes, Small One, honor Him, and in this moment know the answer:

My question: What are God-worshipers like?
Your answer: Arrows aimed at God's bull's-eye.

Psalm 25:12

And now, Beloved, we must journey toward the end of our pathway. The nooks of instruction and knowledge always accessible and drawing, we may return at will, but must leave for interminable moments of flight and fealty. You were created for this moment, Mighty Arrow. Take all that you have learned and fly in the beauty and splendor of His love and majesty.

It is time.

I sought the Lord once again concerning the arrows. I could not help but be saddened at the thought of our coming to the end of this season of training. So much has flowed from His throne in our moments together. Yet, as my flesh tried to move into a place of sorrow, my spirit leapt, as The Archer whispered, *"Buried within the end of each journey...is the beginning of another."*

In my mind's eye, I watched as The Archer of my initial visitation came into view. Walking across a field, He moved with purpose toward a bull's-eye in the middle of tall grasses. A smile upon His face, He stopped just short of the red-centered orb. Something akin to a Father's pleasure crossed His features, followed by full-blown appreciation. His head nodded in approval as He saw the dead-center strike. In my spirit I heard the words, *"Well done!"* as a well-muscled arm extended, hand encircling the shaft of a soundly implanted arrow. I watched as He plucked the small arrow from its mark and lifted it, beginning His examination.

The heart-cry of the arrow reached me: *"I have finished my course, Dear Archer!"* Then, a tug of a smile lifting the corner of His mouth, came the response of The Archer, *"Ah, Little Arrow, that was merely your first flight. A good arrow is used many, many, many..."*

His whisper faded, soft masculine laughter surrounded me, as He walked the field...

Gathering the arrows.

Also Available From

WordCrafts Press

Morning Mist
Stories from the Water's Edge
by Barbie Loflin

I Wish Someone Had Told Me
by Barbie Loflin

Scrambled Hormones
60 Days of Encouragement for Moms Raising Teenage Daughters
by Monica Cane

Youth Ministry is Easy!
and 9 other lies
by Aaron Shaver

Chronicles of a Believer
by Don McCain

Illuminations
by Paula K. Parker & Tracy Sugg

Pro-Verb Ponderings
31 Ruminations on Positive Action
by Rodney Boyd

www.wordcrafts.net